*T*arget *E*nglish

Alan Etherton

Nelson

Thomas Nelson and Sons Ltd
Nelson House Mayfield Road
Walton-on-Thames Surrey
KT12 5PL UK

© Alan Etherton 1995

First published by Thomas Nelson and Sons Ltd 1995

I(T)P Thomas Nelson is an International Thomson Publishing Company
I(T)P is used under licence

ISBN 0-17-433071-5
NPN 9 8 7 6 5 4 3 2

Printed in Croatia

Acknowledgements

The author wishes to acknowledge use of the following copyright material in
Target English:

Extract on p.204 taken from *The Young Warriors* (V S Reid), Longman Caribbean
in association with the Ministry of Education, Jamaica

Extract on p.207 taken from *Annie John* (Jamaica Kincaid)

Contents

Preface

Target English has been written for both native-speakers and for pupils for whom English is a second or foreign language. Depending on the standard of pupils, it can be used in upper primary or lower secondary classes. The book is intended to help pupils to acquire a sound foundation of correct usage and to develop their vocabulary. The main features of the book include:

Part 1: Grammar and Usage

This part of the book is a review of the main uses of all parts of speech. It is based on extensive analyses of the errors made by L1 and L2 learners. It can be used in the classroom and as a reference source for pupils who wish to review language areas at home. The aim of this section is to help pupils to develop a sound foundation from which they can make subsequent progress.

Part 2: Vocabulary

This is an extensive vocabulary section, arranged mainly around common themes, and it serves to develop and consolidate the vocabulary of pupils. Rare words (such as a nide of pheasants and a wisp of snipe) have been excluded because hardly one native-speaking adult in a thousand would recognise or use them. There is no point in burdening pupils with words which they will never use or meet. Both British and American terms have been included.

Part 3: Tests

This section consists of multiple-choice tests of vocabulary and usage. It covers material presented earlier in the book as well as additional items known to be a common source of trouble for pupils.

Part 4: Part 4: Comprehension and Cloze Passages

The ten comprehension passages include work on graphs, charts and tabulated data as well as on traditional prose passages. The section on cloze passages provides guidelines and practice in dealing with passages containing blank spaces, since they are frequently used as a testing device.

A separate teacher's handbook is available from the publishers. This contains the answers to all tests and exercises as well as helpful comments and suggestions.

1 The English Alphabet

These are the letters of the English alphabet:

a b c d e f g h i j k l m n o p q r s t u v w x y z
A B C D E F G H I J K L M N O P Q R S T U V W X Y Z

1.1 Using the alphabet

Check that you know these points:

1 We call 'f' and 'm' letters of the alphabet. The whole alphabet consists of 26 letters, so we NEVER call 'f' and 'm' 'alphabets'.

2 British people pronounce the letter 'z' as 'zed'.
American people pronounce the letter 'z' as 'zee'.

3 When we use 'I' by itself in a sentence, we ALWAYS use a capital letter, e.g.

When I saw my mother, I ran to meet her.
Shall I open the windows?

4 The word for the letter 'h' is 'aitch'. It does not start with 'h', e.g.

He does not speak properly. He leaves the aitch off words such as 'him' and 'her'.

5 Make sure that you can arrange words in alphabetical order. Here are some examples:

1st letter	2nd letter	3rd letter	4th letter
boy	bad	baby	manage
cat	bend	back	mango
dog	bite	badly	Manila
girl	bottle	bag	mankind
loud	butter	bake	manner
pray	by	basin	many

Exercise 1

Arrange the words in each group in alphabetical order.

1 Mary, Susan, Peter, John, Betty, Kate, William, Robert, Tom

2 python, pedal, push, park, piece, point, petal, pole, paper

3 Cheung, Chan, Chin, Chen, church, choose, change, check, chicken

4 settee, seven, settlement, severe, settler, serve, serious, service

1.2   Spelling names on the telephone

Sometimes it is necessary to spell the name of a person or place on the telephone. Then we can use an 'alphabet' like this one:

A – Able	H – House	O – Orange	V – Victor
B – Baby	I – India	P – Peter	W – Window
C – Charlie	J – Jack	Q – Queen	X – X-ray
D – David	K – King	R – Roger	Y – Yankee
E – Easy	L – London	S – Sugar	Z – Zebra
F – Father	M – Mother	T – Tommy	
G – George	N – Norway	U – Uncle	

Mr Oni:	I'd like to book a double room from 5th to 10th May, please.
Clerk:	Yes, sir. What's your name, please?
Mr Oni:	Oreduwa Oni. I'll spell that: Orange, Roger, Easy, David, Uncle, Window, Able, new word, Orange, Norway, India.
Clerk:	Thank you, sir.

Exercise 2

Write down what you can say if you have to spell these names on the telephone.

a Goswami   *b* Szeto   *c* Patti Matsumoto   *d* Frank Pereira

What will you say if you have to spell your own name on the telephone?

Exercise 3

Put in 'a' or 'an'.

1 You have left _____ 'm' out of that word.

2 Put _____ 'u' after the 'o' in this word.

3 That word is spelt wrongly. Put in _____ 'y' after the 't'.

4 There is _____ 's' missing from this word.

5 You have left _____ 'f' out of that word.

6 Don't forget to put _____ 'e' at the end of the word.

7 Make sure you put _____ 'h' at the start of that word next time.

8 Why have you left _____ 'r' out of this word?

9 You have forgotten to put _____ 'b' at the end of this word.

10 I'm sure there's _____ 't' missing from that word.

2   Parts of Speech

2.1   Parts of Speech

Carpenters have names for the tools they use. Similarly, we have names for the tools we use in English. We call them the parts of speech. They are:

nouns	verbs	conjunctions
pronouns	adverbs	exclamations
adjectives	prepositions	

In this chapter, we will take a brief look at them. Then we will study them in detail in later chapters.

2.2   Some words can be used as different parts of speech.

fast

as a noun: People do not eat or drink during a <u>fast</u>.

as an adjective: Malini is a very <u>fast</u> runner.

as a verb: Muslims <u>fast</u> during the month of Ramadan.

as an adverb: My cousin can run very <u>fast</u>.

When we talk about the part of speech of a word, we talk abut the work it does in a sentence. The same word can be a noun in one sentence, an adjective in another sentence, and a verb in a third sentence.

2.3   Nouns

Nouns are the names we give to these things:

something living or without life: a girl, a stone, a desk, a bird, rivers

a quantity or number: a kilometre, miles, a slice, a bunch

feelings, ideas or states: laziness, anger, fear, loneliness

Exercise 1

Put in nouns made from the words in brackets.

1 King Solomon was famous for his _____ (wise).

2 Uncle is a police _____ (inspect) in the Traffic Branch.

3 We must measure the _____ (wide) and _____ (long) of the room before we go to buy a carpet.

4 If Mary wants to go swimming, she has to get _____ (permit) from her mother.

5 Pay _____ (attend)! I'll show you how to do the experiment.

6 What _____ (explain) did he give you for the accident?

7 What's the _____ (high) of that building?

8 Did you have much _____ (difficult) in finding the hospital?

9 Have you been to the Photograph _____ (exhibit)?

10 We have much _____ (please) in enclosing a cheque for $5,000.

2.4   Pronouns

'Pronoun' means 'in place of a noun'. We use a pronoun instead of a noun when we do not want to repeat the noun. Compare these sentences:

with no pronoun: Mary says Mary is going swimming this evening.

with a pronoun: Mary says <u>she</u> is going swimming this evening.

There are different kinds of pronouns. We will study them later in the book. Here are some examples:

1 Would you like something to drink?

2 Are these keys yours or hers?

3 <u>That</u> is Uncle's car. <u>He</u> often leaves books in <u>it</u>.

4 Susan cut <u>herself</u> when <u>she</u> was making some sandwiches.

5 Who told you about the fire that destroyed the shops?

Exercise 2

Choose the right pronouns from the brackets.

1 Peter and (me, I) were nearly late this morning.

2 Mary promised that she would never tell (nobody, anybody) about the mistake.

3 That's not your bag; it's (mine, mines).

4 The keys (that, what) were lost belong to Mr Jansz.

5 When you've finished with the tools, make sure that you put (it, its, them) away safely.

6 This watch is a present from Peter and (I, me).

7 One must learn to defend (myself, oneself).

8 The woman (her, whose, who) car was stolen is very angry.

2.5 Adjectives

We use an adjective to describe or give information about a noun or pronoun.
Adjectives include a, an, the (known as 'articles'), strong, ugly and poor.
We usually put adjectives before a noun or after the verb 'to be':

> Our black kitten is very playful.
> It often chases its tail.

We can use a phrase or a clause instead of an adjective. We put phrases and clauses after a noun or pronoun:

an adjective: The accused man eventually admitted that he had robbed a bank.

a phrase: The man accused of robbery eventually admitted that he had tried to rob a bank.

a clause: The man who was accused of robbery eventually confessed.

Exercise 3

Complete these sentences by making adjectives from the words in brackets.

1 In some countries, it is wise to drink _____ (boil) water.

2 The bus was _____ (crowd) with people, so we could not get a seat.

3 If we are late home, Mother may be _____ (anger) with us.

4 After the robbery, the police were _____ (suspect), so they questioned every member of the staff.

5 My father is a farmer but I am not very _____ (interest) in farming.

6 Pele is a _____ (fame) Brazilian soccer star.

7 _____ (Care) drivers rarely have an accident but _____ (care) ones often do.

8 _____ (Religion) people go to a church, mosque or temple to pray.

9 Switzerland has been a _____ (peace) country for many years.

10 Susan is a very _____ (sense) girl and often looks after young children.

2.6 Verbs

Verbs express an action or (with the verb 'to be') make a statement about a person or thing. Every sentence must have a subject and a verb. The verb must agree with its subject:

singular subjects: My friend lives near me. She is 14 years old.

plural subjects: My friends live near me. They are 14 years old.

Exercise 4

Choose the right word(s) each time.

1 This bunch of bananas _____ heavy.

A is   C are
B has   D look

2 Mary and I _____ to school.

A walking   C walk
B walks   D are walk

3 I _____ your letter two days ago.

A received   C have received
B receiving   D receive

4 Butter _____ in the sun.

A melt   C have melted
B melting   D melts

5 Here _____ two letters for Mother.

A is   C are
B has   D have

6 Tom is absent because he _____ a cold.

A is having   C have
B has   D will have

7 All of this furniture
_____ new

  A is   C looking
  B look   D are

8 It's late. It's time we
_____ home.

  A go   C went
  B going   D gone

9 I wonder where Ann and
Sue _____ now.

  A is   C were
  B have   D are

10 What time _____
the show start?

  A does   C has
  B is   D was

2.7   Adverbs

Adverbs give us information about the action of a verb. For example, they often tell us how something is done: quickly, slowly, lazily, well, etc. They can also modify an adjective or another adverb.

with a verb: Mr King drives carefully.

with an adjective: He is a very careful man.

with an adverb: His wife also drives very carefully.

Sometimes we use an adverb phrase or clause instead of an adverb:

with an adverb: The taxi stopped <u>here</u>.

with a phrase: The taxi stopped outside this building.

with a clause: It stopped where we are standing now.

Exercise 5

Choose the best word(s) each time.

1 Mary can swim very
_____ now.

  A good   C skilful
  B well   D quick

2 Our house is small but we all
live _____ together.

  A happy   C happily
  B happiness

3 My father works
_____ and often
comes home _____
at night.

  A hardly ... lately

  B hardly ... late
  C hard ... lately
  D hard ... late

4 Make sure that you are
sitting _____ .

  A comfortable
  B comforting
  C comfort
  D comfortably

5 Sometimes the music on
television is very
_____ .

  A loudly   B loud

6 During the fire, a young girl jumped from a window. _____ for her, two firemen caught her.

A Lucky   B Luckily

7 My sister did very _____ in her test.

A good   B well

8 When the storm arrived, the spectators _____ ran for shelter.

A hurry   C hurrying
B hurried   D hurriedly

9 That was a _____ day for all of us.

A badly   B bad

10 The refugees felt _____ and _____ when the rebels advanced towards their camp.

A lonely ... helpless
B lonely ... helplessly
C alone ... hopelessly
D alone ... hoping

2.8 Prepositions

Prepositions are used to show the manner, place or time of an action:

manner	with great care	in a hurry	at great speed
place	under the table	on the chair	by the door
time	before six thirty	in the evening	on Saturday morning

Remember that we use an object pronoun (me, him, her, us, them) after a preposition.

a This is a secret between you and <u>me</u>.

b When you see Devi, please give this parcel to <u>her</u>.

Exercise 6

Choose the right words from the brackets.

1 Mother is going to Kingston (in, on) Saturday morning.

2 Our neighbour is a security guard. He works (in, at, during) night.

3 When we were going towards Port of Spain, a car came round a bend (in, with, at) a great speed and narrowly missed colliding (at, with) a lorry going (to, in, for) the opposite direction.

4 This watch is slightly different (from, than, to) yours.

5 It is (out of, against, contrary) the law to steal things from shops.

6 I'll stay at home this evening. No, (on, at, with) second thoughts, I'll go with you.

7 Mother will be annoyed (to, with, at) us, if we lose our money.

8 Susan cut her hand (on, to, by) the sharp edge of a tin can.

9 When John returned (back, to, –) home, he changed his shirt.

10 My sister is going to marry (–, with) her boyfriend (in, at) the end of the month.

2.9   Conjunctions

Conjunctions are linking words such as <u>and,</u> <u>but,</u> <u>because,</u> <u>so</u> and although.

In most cases, only ONE conjunction is used to join expressions:

a Although the dress was expensive, Mary decided to buy it.

b We could not get on the bus <u>because</u> it was full already.

2.10   Exclamations

We use exclamations such as <u>Oh!</u> and <u>Ow!</u> to show a strong feeling such as pain, surprise or happiness.

a What a kind girl!

b Ow! That injection hurt!

c Ugh! Look at that huge spider. I hope it's not poisonous.

Note   In the following chapters, we will study the parts of speech in greater detail.

3   Nouns

1 Plurals	*6* Ending in 's'	*11* Compound	*14* (Un)count-able
2 Gender	*7* -ce, -se	*12* Adjectives as nouns	*15* Classifiers
3 Common	*8* Proper	*13* Nouns as adjectives	*16* Formation
4 Possession	*9* Collective		
5 No plural	*10* Abstract		

3.1   Plurals

The plural form of nouns can be made in these ways:

1 add 's' (pronounced /s/ as in 'so')

shop – shops	sock – socks	cliff – cliffs
cat – cats	book – books	cup – cups

2 add 's' (pronounced /z/ as in 'zoo')

girl – girls	boy – boys	window – windows
door – doors	eye – eyes	bottle – bottles

3 add 'es' (pronounced /iz/)

race – races	box – boxes	match – matches
dish – dishes	tax – taxes	church – churches

4 add 's' or 'es' to words ending in 'o'

-os: pianos, photos, radios, ratios, cellos, hippos, memos, solos

-oes: tomatoes, potatoes, mosquitoes, heroes, dominoes, buffaloes

-os or -oes: mango(e)s, banjo(e)s

As a rough guide, if somebody or something can <u>eat</u> something which ends in 'o', the plural form is probably -oes.

5 (sometimes) change final 'f' or 'fe' to 'ves'

-ves: leaves, wives, thieves, knives, halves, calves, loaves, shelves, wolves

-fs: cliffs, handkerchiefs, chiefs, safes (in a bank or home), roofs

6 add 's' if a word ends in a vowel letter plus 'y'

key – keys   day – days   donkey – donkeys

monkey – monkeys valley – valleys   turkey – turkeys

7 If a noun ends in a consonant + 'y', take off the 'y' and add 'ies'.

baby – babies   lady – ladies   diary – diaries

fairy – fairies   body – bodies   city – cities

8 Change final 'is' to 'es'.

oasis – oases   crisis – crises   basis – bases

9 Use -en. This is an old plural form and is used for a few words only.

man – men   woman – women   child – children

ox – oxen   brother – brethren (rare)
                      (or) brothers

10 A few nouns have an irregular plural form which includes a change of vowel.

tooth – teeth   mouse – mice

goose – geese   louse – lice

11 Some English words come from Latin or Greek. They may have irregular plural forms.

medium – media   bacterium – bacteria

index – indexes or indices   appendix – appendixes or
                                  appendices

12 Check that you know the plural form of the following words.

brother-in-law – brothers-in-law   spoonful – spoonfuls

son-in-law – sons-in-law   cupful – cupfuls

passer-by – passers-by   mouse-trap – mouse-traps

Exercise 1

What is the plural form of these words?

1 ferry	*4* bully	*7* lady	*10* mosquito	*13* reef
2 story	*5* trolley	*8* leaf	*11* photo	*14* army
3 storey	*6* theory	*9* woman	*12* classroom	*15* knife

3.2   Gender

masculine: boy, son, father, grandfather, nephew, bull, ram, dog, tom-cat (males)

feminine: girl, daughter, mother, grandmother, niece, cow, ewe, bitch, she-cat (females)

common: baby, doctor, teacher, friend, parent, relative, guardian, cousin (may be male or female)

neuter: book, ceiling, radio, dirt, lorry, fan, knife, mirror, sausage (not male or female)

Sailors refer to their ship as 'ship' and 'her'. A few motorists (who are very fond of their car) refer to their car as 'she' and 'her'. Most ordinary people refer to a ship or car as 'it'.

PEOPLE

Masculine	Feminine	Masculine	Feminine
abbot	abbess	giant	giantess
actor	actress	god	goddess
bachelor	spinster	grandfather	grandmother
baron	baroness	he	she
beau	belle	headmaster	headmistress
boy	girl	heir	heiress
brave	squaw	hero	heroine
bridegroom	bride	him(self)	her(self)
brother	sister	host	hostess
conductor	conductress	husband	wife
count	countess	Irishman	Irish woman
deacon	deaconess	Jew	Jewess
duke	duchess	king	queen
earl	countess	lad	lass
emperor	empress	landlord	landlady
executor	executrix	lord	lady
father	mother	male	female
fiancé	fiancée	man	woman
Filipino	Filipina	manager	manageress
gentleman	lady	marquis	marchioness

13

Masculine	Feminine	Masculine	Feminine
masseur	masseuse	prophet	prophetess
master	mistress	proprietor	proprietrix
mayor	mayoress	sir	madam, miss
monk	nun	Sir	Lady
Mr (married)	Mrs (married)	son	daughter
Mr (unmarried)	Miss (unmarried)	son-in-law	daughter-in-law
Mr (We don't know if he is married or not.)	Ms (we don't know if she is married or not.)	spokesman	spokeswoman
		step-father	step-mother
		step-son	step-daughter
murderer	murderess	steward	stewardess
nephew	niece	sultan	sultana
papa	mama	tailor	tailoress dressmaker
patron	patroness		
peer	peeress	traitor	traitress
poet	poet(ess)	tutor	governess
policeman	policewoman	uncle	aunt
postman	postwoman	waiter	waitress
priest	priestess	widower	widow
prince	princess	wizard	witch

ANIMALS

Masculine	Feminine	Masculine	Feminine
billy-goat	nanny-goat	gander	goose
boar	sow	jackass	jenny-ass
buck	doe	lion	lioness
bull	cow	peacock	peahen
bullock	heifer	ram	ewe
cob (swan)	pen	sire	dam
cock(erel)	hen	stag	hind
colt	filly	stallion	mare
dog	bitch	steer	heifer
drake	duck	tiger	tigress
fox	vixen	tom-cat	she-cat

Exercise 2

What are the feminine of the following?

1 a bridegroom	*4* a policeman	*7* a Filipino	*10* a tiger
2 a widower	*5* a husband	*8* a landlord	*11* a stallion
3 a hero	*6* a nephew	*9* a dog	*12* a bull elephant

Exercise 3

What are the masculine of the following?

1 a doe rabbit	*4* a mare	*7* Ms	*10* brides
2 a ewe	*5* a duck	*8* women	*11* spinster
3 a vixen	*6* an aunt	*9* heroines	*12* hers

3.3　Common nouns

The main types of nouns are common nouns, collective nouns, proper nouns and abstract nouns. A common noun is the name of one thing (or person) from a group or class, e.g. a girl, a car, a tree, a spider, a shark, a television set. Most nouns are common nouns.

3.4　Possession

When we use an apostrophe to show possession, we follow these rules:

a Put 's after a singular noun or a plural noun which does NOT end in 's'.

> my uncle's car – the car of my uncle
> the fishermen's net – the net belonging to the fishermen

b Put an apostrophe after a plural noun which ends in 's'.

> my friends' bicycles – the bicycles of my friends
> the players' entrance – the entrance for players

c If a singular name ends in 's', you can add 's or only an apostrophe (whichever you prefer).

> Charles's wife – Charles' wife – the wife of Charles

> In most cases, we use an apostrophe when we are writing about people or common animals, but it is also used in these expressions:

an hour's delay	a nation's army	the sun's rays
two weeks' holiday	Brazil's forest	a day's pay
in a month's time	a country's exports	the earth's surface

When we write or speak about things which are not people or common animals, we normally use 'of' and not an apostrophe:

at the back of the bus	the side of the lorry
the end of the path	the top of the page

We can use an apostrophe for a contraction such as I'm and they've but we do not put an apostrophe at the end of a verb.

Exercise 4

Choose the right word(s) from the brackets.

1 Uncle _____ (lives, live's, lives') near us and often _____ (comes, comes', come's) to see us. I know that _____ (Uncles, Uncle, Uncle's) car is newer than _____ (ours, ours').

2 The _____ (taxi's front, front of the taxi) was damaged in the collision. One of the _____ (passenger's, passengers, passengers') was slightly hurt but her _____ (injuries, injuries') are not serious. She should be all right in a few (days, day's, days') time.

3 Sometimes we can see _____ (swings, swing's, swings') and _____ (slide's, slides', slides) in a _____ (childrens, children's, childrens') park.

   day I helped my friend to repair her bicycle. There were two _____ (punctures, puncture's, punctures') in one of the (wheels, wheel's, wheels'). We finished the job in about ten _____ (minutes, minute's, minutes').

3.5 Nouns with no plural form

1 Some words have the same form for both singular and plural. They include deer, fish (also fishes), aircraft, sheep, salmon, cod and trout.

2 Do not add an 's' to these words:

apparatus	equipment	housework	scenery
baggage	everything	information	slang
blood	evidence	laughter	thunder
bread	excitement	luggage	traffic
charcoal	fiction	make-up	vegetation
Chinese	firewood	mud	*work (to do)
clothing	the following	music	woodwork
dictation	fun	poetry	**damage
dirt	furniture	punctuation	
drizzle	gold	rainfall	
dust	homework	rice	

* We can add an 's' to 'work' when we refer to things created by a writer, poet, artist, sculptor or similar person. ** We can add 's' to 'damage' when we refer to money paid as compensation, e.g. 'damages for breaking a contract'.

3.6   Do not leave off the final 's'

Do not leave off the final 's' in these words:

a lens in a camera	our surroundings	give our regards to her
to make friends with	in low spirits	congratulations on your win
a means to an end	in other words	a plastics factory
to take pains to do	nowadays	on good terms with her
on second thoughts	mathematics	pay your respects to
burst into tears	the news	the proceeds of a sale
her belongings	at headquarters	*the first innings
in a barracks	a summons	her earnings

*Many Americans refer to 'the first/second inning'. They also use math and not maths as the short form of 'mathematics'.

3.7 Practice and practise

In British English (but not in American English), we use -ce for a noun, and -se for a verb in the following pairs of words.

nouns: practice advice licence device prophecy

verbs: practise advise license devise prophesy

a Have you got a driving licence yet?

b Is your uncle licensed to sell gold and silver?

c You need a lot of practice to play a guitar well.

d John practises playing his guitar every evening.

3.8 Proper nouns

Proper nouns start with a capital letter. They are the names of people, cities, countries, seas and oceans, mountains, rivers, hotels, newspapers, etc. Each noun refers to a particular person or thing. Examples include Peter, Bermuda, Kenya, Zimbabwe, Nigeria, Malta, MV Morning Star, the Mediterranean, etc.

Exercise 5

In each line, which words should start with a capital letter when we use them inside a sentence?

1 happiness, gold, holiday, jamaica, january, zambia, indonesia, mary, famous

2 diamonds, death, bread, sugar, concrete, atlantic ocean, asia, singapore

3 thailand, his sister, susan tan, president clinton, australia, hong kong, tokyo

4 difficulty, news, headquarters, plastics, physical, dear, your, chinese, water

5 poem, television, saturday, october, rainfall, graph, climate, experiment

3.9 Collective nouns

A collective noun is the name of a group of persons or things. Examples include:

an army of soldiers	a group of islands, musicians
an audience of people	a herd of cattle, deer
a band of musicians	a jury of people
a board of directors	a litter of puppies, kittens
a choir of singers	a majority of voters, answers
a class of pupils	a mob of people
a committee of people	a nation of people
a congregation of people	a pack of cards, lies, wolves
a crew of a ship, plane	the public
a crowd of people	a school of whales
a family of people	a shoal of fish
a fleet of ships, planes, cars	a staff of employees
a flock of birds, sheep	a swam of bees
a gang of thieves, criminals	a team of players
a government of citizens	a tribe of people

We regard a collective noun as singular if we are thinking of the group as a whole.

a This committee is a temporary one and will soon finish its work.

b The audience is a large one tonight.

If we are referring to individuals within a group, we regard a collective noun as plural:

c The committee have decided that they will discuss the plan on Monday.

d The audience are clapping their hands and stamping their feet.

3.10 Abstract nouns

These nouns are the names of qualities, actions or states, e.g. kindness, bravery, laughter, hatred, slavery, sleep, poverty, etc. Normally these nouns have no plural form and we do not use 'a', 'an' or 'the' before them unless the noun is described by following words.

Nobody likes to talk about death.
Nobody wanted to talk about the death of the taxi-driver.

3.11 Compound nouns

These nouns are made by joining two shorter words, e.g. head-mistress, classroom, eyelid, stomach-ache, football and waterfall.

Exercise 6

Take words from each list to form new compound nouns.

List A: water, head, hand, eye, eye, foot, rain, rail, life, arm, post

List B: cuff, brow, man, hole, bow, way, sight, ache, ball, fall, belt,

3.12 Adjectives used as nouns

Words such as poor, rich, blind, deaf and wealthy are normally used as adjectives. When we use them as nouns, they refer to a large group. We never add an 's' to them but we use a plural verb with them.

a The rich are not worried about the increase in the price of petrol but the poor have been badly affected by it.

b The blind and deaf are at a disadvantage when they seek jobs.

3.13 Nouns used as adjectives

Many nouns can be used as adjectives. Then we normally use the singular form of the noun, e.g.

a shoe shop	a paint company	some fish soup
a watch factory	a book store	some chicken curry

Sometimes we use a plural noun, e.g. a clothes shop.

3.14 Countable and uncountable nouns

a We cannot count such things as dirt, dust, smoke and water, so we call them uncountable (or mass) nouns.

b We can count things such as chairs, dollars, bags and keys, so we call them countable nouns.

Study the following tables. Learn which words we can use before each type of noun. You will see that '(not) a lot of' is useful because we can use it before both countable and uncountable nouns.

Countable nouns		Uncountable nouns	
(not) many	people	(not) much	meat
a few	cars	a little	rice
(not) a lot of	birds	(not) a lot of	dirt
a number of	books	an amount of	smoke
		a quantity of	maize

Exercise 7

Choose the right words from the brackets.

1 Mary: Do you have _____ (many, much) money left, John?

John: No, only a _____ (few, little) cents.

2 Susan: Did you see _____ (many, much) women at the meeting?

Anne: Yes, quite a _____ (little, few). There were quite a _____ (little, few) girls there, too.

3 The firemen had difficulty fighting the fire because there was a large _____ (number, amount) of smoke.

4 Do you have _____ (many, much) homework to do this evening?

No, not _____ (many, much) but I have a _____ (few, little) difficult problems to solve.

5 Don't forget to put a _____ (few, little) salt in those vegetables but don't put too _____ (many , much) in.

3.15 Classifiers

We can use classifiers (or 'measure words') with countable and uncountable nouns. Here are some examples:

Countable Nouns	Uncountable Nouns
a bottle of mango slices	a bale of rubber/cotton/paper
a box/tin of biscuits/chocolates	a bar of soap/chocolate/steel/gold
a bunch of bananas/grapes/flowers	a drop of blood/water/milk/petrol
a bundle of clothes/sticks	a loaf of bread
a carton of cigarettes	a lump of mud/clay/dough
a collection of stamps/shells	a pane of glass
a container of plastic toys	a piece of chalk/bread/meat/paper
a crate of new typewriters	a reel of cotton/thread
a litter of kittens/puppies	a roll of cloth
a packet of corn flakes	a sack of rice/cement/sand
a pair of scissors/trousers	a sheet of paper/glass
a group of spectators/girls	a slice of bread/pineapple/cucumber

3.16 Forming nouns

Common noun endings include the following:

age baggage, village, package, carriage, advantage, language, damage

al approval, burial, dial, equal, funeral, rehearsal, rival, trial

ance allowance, ambulance, appliance, attendance, balance, endurance

ar, er, or beggar, burglar, driver, swimmer, actor, inspector, doctor

ence absence, silence, difference, patience, experience, audience

ery bravery, bribery, delivery, discovery, machinery, robbery, scenery

ian librarian, barbarian, guardian, musician, civilian, electrician

ing walking, swimming, running, beginning, ceiling, drawing, clothing

ist cyclist, motorist, artist, biologist, dentist, pianist, tourist

ity ability, charity, electricity, majority, opportunity, similarity

man policeman, postman, fireman, fisherman, salesman, sportsman, seaman

ment	government, argument, employment, enjoyment, equipment, experiment
ness	kindness, happiness, business, hardness, politeness, witness
ship	friendship, scholarship, membership, relationship, citizenship
sion	collision, confession, decision, division, explosion, invasion
th	width, length, breadth, depth, health, strength, warmth, wealth
tion	attention, action, attraction, collection, education, dictation
ty	safety, cruelty, difficulty, honesty, liberty, poverty, loyalty
ure	pleasure, treasure, leisure, creature, departure, picture, nature
y	baby, city, lady, fairy, army, apology, academy, filly, holly

Exercise 8

Make nouns from the following words:

1 wide	*6* encourage	*11* disappoint	*16* brave
2 deep	*7* foreign	*12* pronounce	*17* wise
3 true	*8* travel	*13* exclaim	*18* refuse
4 safe	*9* correct	*14* decide	*19* marry
5 employ	*10* warn	*15* agree	*20* short

Exercise 9

Correct any mistakes in these sentences.

1 Finish all your homeworks before you go out to play with your friends!

2 We were studying punctuations in our lesson before the recess.

3 Have all the damages to the car been repaired yet?

4 I have just made friend with a new girl in our class.

5 The headquarter of the soldiers is at a barrack on the outskirts of the town.

6 Miss King has received a summon to appear in court in a weeks time.

7 The len in this camera is no good; you must get another one.

8 Mary burst into tear when she heard the sad new of John's death.

9 If you want to learn to play the piano good, you must practice often.

10 A thermostat is a devise for controlling the temperature of something.

Exercise 10

Correct any mistakes in these sentences.

1 Is that Uncles car or Mr Youngs?

2 When we went swimming, we left all our clothings on the beach.

3 Last week I saw several Japaneses inspecting a site for a factory.

4 Find any mistakes in the followings and correct it.

5 Most of the traffics on this road stop at night.

6 Some african countries have been badly affected by drought and by other problem.

7 On a plane, the flight crew consist of the pilot, co-pilot and flight engineer.

8 The jury are just coming back to its seats.

9 Don't forget that february is the shortest Month of the year.

10 If taxes are increased, the poors will be affected.

4 Pronouns

1 Personal	*4* Reflexive and	*6* Indefinite
2 Possessive	Emphasizing	*7* Relative (1)
3 Demonstrative	*5* Interrogative	*8* Relative (2)

4.1 Personal Pronouns

We saw in section 2.4 that pronouns are used in place of a noun.
These are the Personal Pronouns:

as the subject: I   he   she   it   we   you   they

as the object or
after a preposition: me   him   her   it   us   you   them

Points to remember:

a Use an object pronoun after a preposition.

Between you and me, he has made a mistake.

This watch is a present from Mary and me.

b Put yourself last: My friend and I – NOT I and my friend.

c British and American usage is not always the same.

question: Who's there?

answer: (British, Me. or It's me.

(American) It's I.

d Make sure that your pronoun agrees with the word it
replaces or refers to.

Exercise 1

Choose the right words from the brackets.

1 Last Sunday, _____ (I and my sister, my sister and I) went to the cinema.

2 My mother had some heavy bags, so I helped _____ (she, he, him, her) to carry _____ (it, its, them, they) home.

3 Sometimes Uncle takes my brother and _____ (I, me) to school.

4 My friend and _____ (I, me) went fishing yesterday.

5 I saw a lot of weeds, so I pulled _____ (it, they, them) up and threw _____ (them, it, they) away.

6 At six o'clock, _____ (I with my sister, my sister with me, my sister and I) decided that it was time for _____ (us, we) to go home.

7 I saw a woman drop some keys, so I picked _____ (her, it, them) up and gave _____ (its, they, them) to _____ (she, her, him).

8 A policeman saw my brother and _____ (me, I), so he stopped _____ (we, us) and wanted to know where _____ (they, us, we) were going.

9 When we approached my friend's home, we saw that _____ (they, it, its) was on fire.

10 Don't leave your clothes there. Put _____ (them, him, it) away neatly.

4.2 Possessive Pronouns

The possessive pronouns are shown underlined below. They replace a noun and another word. We never put an apostrophe on a possessive pronoun.

This is my key.	It is mine.
That is your key.	It is yours.
This is Tom's pen.	It is his.
That is Sue's pen.	It is hers.
This is our car.	It is ours.
That is their cat.	It is theirs.

4.3 Demonstrative Pronouns

We call this, these, that and those demonstrative pronouns when they are used without a following noun. They show which person(s) or thing(s) somebody is referring to.

a This is your pen. That is my pen.

b I think these are your shoes; those are probably Mary's.

4.4 Reflexive and Emphasizing Pronouns

Reflexive and emphasizing pronouns have the same form but are used in different ways. They are shown below:

singular	plural
I enjoyed myself at the party.	We all enjoyed ourselves.
Don't hurt yourself, John.	Don't hurt yourselves, boys.
Mary cut herself by accident.	They cut themselves by accident.
Peter nearly hurt himself.	
Our cat often washes itself.	
One must defend oneself at times.	

None of these pronouns ends in fs.

a Reflexive pronouns often follow a verb or preposition. The action of the verb is 'reflected' back to the subject.

1   Vimala blamed herself for the mistake.

2   Susan and Devi moved the furniture by themselves.

Exercise 2

Put in suitable reflexive pronouns.

1 My sister weighed _____

2 I dried _____ with a towel.

3 The dog scratched _____

4 He taught _____ to swim.

5 He defended _____

6 I measured _____

7 We really enjoyed _____ at the picnic.

8 The cat stood up and stretched _____

9 People sometimes weigh _____ in the morning.

10 Make sure you behave _____ boys.

b Emphasizing pronouns usually follow a noun or pronoun to emphasize something.

    1   The story must be true because Mrs King told me about it _____.

    2   The district where they live is not very nice but the house _____ is excellent.

Exercise 3

Put in suitable emphasizing pronouns.

1 I know the news is correct. Mrs Oni _____ told me.

2 Peter and Anne enjoyed the film but I _____ didn't much like it.

3 Don't interfere, Susan. Let the boys _____ settle the argument.

4 Mrs Menon: What do you think of this picture?

    Mr Menon: Well, the picture _____ is very good but the frame is rather shabby.

5 The fire affected several flats but we _____ were hardly affected by it.

6 Anne: How do you know that they're going to get married?

    Sue: Vimala _____ told me, so it must be true. She's going to be the bride.

7 Sarjit: How did you know that Devi is going to Kingston next week?

    Daljit: You've got a poor memory. You _____ told me last week.

8 We were lucky not to lose the game but the players _____ expected to win easily.

4.5 Interrogative Pronouns

These pronouns are used at the start of a question:

Who found your ring?   What is that strange machine for?

Whose is the watch?   Which of them is the cheaper?

Whom did you speak to?

Exercise 4

In each blank space, put in one of the five interrogative pronouns above.

1 I wonder who this car belongs to? Ask Mary _____ it is.

2 _____ are those big pieces of wood for? Are you going to repair something?

3 Uncle gave me these two watches. _____ of them do you want?

4 Let me see that letter! To _____ is it addressed?

5 _____ gave you the letter? Did you get it from the postman?

6 _____ is this camera? It's a nice one.

7 Mary wants to know _____ is in this locked box.

8 _____ is the answer to question 4? Is my answer correct?

9 _____ are those two ladies in the back of the car? I've never seen them before.

10 Susan wants to know _____ of those women has come from Thailand.

4.6 Indefinite Pronouns

We call these words indefinite pronouns. They do not refer to a definite person or thing.

anybody	everybody	nobody	somebody
anyone	everyone	no one	someone
anything	everything	nothing	something

a The words ending with 'one' are similar in meaning to those ending in 'body'.

Was there anyone there? = Was there anybody there?

b Except for 'no one', all the pronouns are single words.

c We can often put 'else' after one of the pronouns:

Is there anything else to eat?
Did you score the goal or did somebody else get it?

d If one of the pronouns is the subject, we use a singular verb after it.

Everything is ready. Everybody is waiting for you.

4.7   Relative Pronouns (1)

Relative pronouns are used to link two statements about a person or thing.

1a I know the girl. She won the first prize.

1b I know the girl who won the first prize. (or use 'that')

2a That is the shop. It caught fire last night.

2b That is the shop which caught fire last night. (or use 'that')

The relative pronouns are who, that, which, whose and whom. This is how we can use them:

who + a verb   We use 'who' to refer to people (and not to things). It is the subject of the verb which follows it, as in 1b above.

People who live in glass houses should not throw stones.

The girl who sits next to me can speak four languages.

Do you know the woman who owns that shop?

which + a verb We use 'which' to refer to things (and not to people). It is the subject of the verb which follows it, as in 2b above.

Animals which attack people are usually killed.

The storm which came during the night flooded two homes.

Where is the parcel which arrived this morning?

that + a verb　　We can use 'that' to refer to people or things. It can replace 'who' or 'which' in the sentences above.

Exercise 5

Use who, which or that and use the information in each pair of sentences to make one sentence each time. You may have to add or omit some words. If you are not sure what to do, study 1a, 1b, 2a and 2b at the start of this section.

1 Here comes the boy. He found the money.

2 That is the policewoman. She stopped Uncle's car.

3 The storm came during the night. It knocked down several trees.

4 That is the bend. It probably caused the accident.

5 Some people live near the sea. They can usually swim well.

6 A vet is a man or woman. He or she can help sick or injured animals.

7 Wheat, maize and rice are important crops. They keep billions of people alive.

8 Adolf Hitler was the German leader. He started World War II.

9 Joseph Stalin was a Russian leader. He controlled the USSR for several years.

10 A bus broke down. It was soon repaired.

whose + a noun　　We can use 'whose' to show possession or that something is part of a person or thing.

I know the man whose car was damaged.

The player whose leg was injured was carried off the field.

4.8　Relative Pronouns (2)

In some sentences, a relative pronoun is the object of a verb. Then it is often left out, especially in speech.

1a This is the watch. Uncle gave me it.

1b This is the watch which/that Uncle gave me. (Omit 'it'.)

1c This is the watch Uncle gave me.

2a I know the girl. A taxi hit her.

2b I know the girl whom a taxi hit. (Omit 'her'.)

2c I know the girl a taxi hit.

Exercise 6

Use the information in each pair of sentences to make one sentence.
You can make sentences like those in 1b and 2b or like those in 1c and 2c.

1 Where is the parcel? Uncle brought it.

2 I've lost the pen. You gave me it last week.

3 What's the name of the girl? Mary invited her to the party.

4 That's the woman. We spoke to her last night.

5 Where have you put the letter? Mrs King sent it last week.

5   Adjectives

1 Proper	*3* nce/nt	*5* Uses 1	*7* + prepositions
2 ed/ing	*4* Comparison	*6* Uses 2	*8* Formation

Please see 3.12 for adjectives used as nouns, and see 3.13 for nouns used as adjectives.

5.1   Proper Adjectives

We make proper adjectives from proper nouns. They show the place or nationality of a noun.

Proper Noun	Proper Adjective	Proper Noun	Proper Adjective
Africa	African	Jordan	Jordanian
Australia	Australian	Kenya	Kenyan
Barbados	Barbadian	Korea	Korean
Belgium	Belgian	Lebanon	Lebanese

Proper Noun	Proper Adjective	Proper Noun	Proper Adjective
Belize	Belizean	Malaysia	Malaysian
Brazil	Brazilian	Malta	Maltese
Britain	British	Mauritus	Mauritian
Canada	Canadian	Mexico	Mexican
China	Chinese	New Zealand	New Zealand
Denmark	Danish	Nigeria	Nigerian
Egypt	Egyptian	Norway	Norwegian
England	English	Pakistan	Pakistani
Europe	European	Philippines	Philippine
Finland	Finnish	Poland	Polish
France	French	Portugal	Portuguese
Germany	German	Russia	Russian
Ghana	Ghanaian	Saudi Arabia	Saudi Arabian
Greece	Greek	Scotland	Scottish
Grenada	Grenadian	Singapore	Singaporean
Guyana	Guyanese	Spain	Spanish
Holland	Dutch	St Kitts	Kittitian
Hungary	Hungarian	St Lucia	St Lucian
Iceland	Icelandic	St Vincent	Vincentian
India	Indian	Sweden	Swedish
Indonesia	Indonesian	Switzerland	Swiss
Iran	Iranian	Thailand	Thai
Iraq	Iraqi	Trinidad	Trinidadian
Ireland (Eire)	Irish	Turkey	Turkish
Israel	Israeli	USA	American
Italy	Italian	Wales	Welsh
Jamaica	Jamaican	Zambia	Zambian
Japan	Japanese	Zimbabwe	Zimbabwean

Note: The above adjectives are NOT always used for citizens of a country. For example, a British person is a Briton. A Spanish person is a Spaniard.

Exercise 1

Put in adjectives formed from the words in brackets.

1 Mr Richards is a famous _____ cricketer. (Antigua)

2 For many years _____ asphalt has been exported to Europe. (Trinidad)

3 This furniture was made from _____ mahogany. (Belize)

4 Many people think that _____ watches are the best. (Switzerland)

5 A lot of people own a _____ television set or camera. (Japan)

6 Uncle has gone on a _____ safari. (Zimbabwe)

7 A lot of _____ people live in the capital, Bangkok. (Thailand)

8 At one time, the _____ eagle was known as the monkey-eating eagle. (the Philippines)

9 _____ whisky is well known throughout the world. (Scotland)

10 For many years, _____ rum has also been well known. (Jamaica)

5.2 Adjectives ending in -ed or -ing

There are many pairs of adjectives which end in -ed or -ing, e.g.

-ed excited, interested, bored, annoyed, boiled, surprised

-ing exciting, interesting, boring, annoying, boiling, surprising

a Adjectives ending in -ed show what has happened to a person or thing.

b Adjectives ending in -ing show the effect which something has on a person or thing.

Imagine that you are watching a film on television. If the film is good, it will be interesting. You will be interested in it. If the film is boring, you will be bored.

A useful guideline is '-ed for people; -ing for things'. This is only a rough guide but it is useful for common pairs of adjectives.

Exercise 2

Put in the -ed or -ing form of the words in brackets.

1 John was _____ (annoy) when he missed the last bus and had to walk home.

2 Have you read the book *Jurassic Park?* It is very _____ (interest), especially if you are _____ (interest) in science and biology.

3 What an _____ (annoy) mistake! Father won't be _____ (please).

4 Mother was _____ (annoy) when she left her keys inside the car.

5 The result of the game was quite _____ (surprise). The weaker team won.

6 Mary thinks soccer matches are _____ (bore) and never watches them.

7 Mrs Nathan was _____ (puzzle) and _____ (annoy) when firemen arrived at her home to put out a non-existent fire.

8 A plane flew low over our house, making a _____ (deafen) noise.

5.3 Adjectives ending in -nt

In pairs of words like those below, nouns end in -nce. Adjectives end in -nt.

noun: difference silence absence importance obedience ignorance

adjective: different   silent   absent   important   obedient   ignorant

Note: 'Assistant', 'equivalent' and 'patient' can be adjectives or nouns.

Exercise 3

Choose the right words from the brackets.

1 What's the (difference, different) between these two stamps?

2 This one is (difference, different) from that one because it has been used.

3 People who use a library should be (silence, silent) and should not cause (inconvenience, inconvenient) to others.

4 At first, John's (absence, absent) from the weekly meetings was not noticed but eventually somebody commented on his (absence, absent).

5 Will 10.30 be (convenience, convenient) for you? If it is (inconvenience, inconvenient), we can arrange a (difference, different) time for you.

6 Young children sometimes get into trouble if they are (disobedient, disobedience).

7 (Negligence, negligent) often causes accidents.

8 If a worker is (negligence, negligent), he may lose his job.

5.4   Comparison of adjectives

We can make comparisons with adjectives in these ways:

	Positive (one only)	Comparative (one of two only)	Superlative (one of three or more)
group (i)	tall smart strong	taller smarter stronger	tallest smartest strongest
group (ii)	expensive awkward difficult	more expensive more awkward more difficult	most expensive most awkward most difficult
group (iii)	good bad far little } small }	better worse farther smaller	best worst farthest smallest

Group (i):   This method of comparison is used for most adjectives of one syllable.
It is also used for some adjectives with two or more syllables.

Group (ii):   This form of comparison, with more or most, is used for all other adjectives except the few irregular ones in group (iii).

Important notes:

a We never put 'more' before an adjective AND add -er to its end. Similarly, we never use both 'most' and -est with an adjective.

b In theory, superlative adjectives are used when we compare one of three or more people or things. In practice, many English people do not bother about how many things they are comparing. If they want to compare one thing with one, two or fifty others, they use the comparative. If they want to speak about the biggest, best or most expensive, they use the superlative even when they are speaking about two things only, e.g.

(i)   Put your best foot forward. (We have only two feet.)

(ii) May the best man win. (There may be only two men fighting.)

(iii) I like both the cars but this one is the cheapest.(Two cars.)

Your teacher will tell you whether to follow the theoretical method or not.

Exercise 4

Give the comparative and superlative of these adjectives:

1 kind	*6* poor	*11* generous	*16* careful
2 horrible	*7* bad	*12* intelligent	*17* great
3 beautiful	*8* good	*13* attractive	*18* expensive
4 thin	*9* tidy	*14* hard	*19* comfortable
5 pretty	*10* helpful	*15* little	*20* noisy

Exercise 5

Put in the correct form of the adjectives in brackets.

1 Travelling by air is (fast) but (expensive) than travelling by sea.

2 A kilometre is (short) than a mile but much (long) than a metre.

3 Watching the television is (good) than listening to the radio.

4 Mary's new watch is (accurate) than her old one but it was (expensive).

5 February is the (short) month of the year. In Europe, it is also the (cold).

6 Many people say that women are (careful) drivers than men.

7 All these photos are very good. This one is (good) than that one. The (good) of them all is the one at the end.

8 John felt ill on Monday, (bad) on Tuesday, and (bad) on Wednesday. Then he began to recover and felt much (good) on Saturday.

5.5 Uses of adjectives (1)

a How + an adjective!

    1 How kind of you to come! We're delighted to see you.

    2 How strange! Are you sure that story is true?

b as + adjective + as

    1 Bermuda is not as big as Jamaica.

    2 Silver is not as valuable or as scarce as gold.

c so + adjective + that

    1 We were so tired that we decided to go to bed early.

    2 Last night it was so hot that we could not sleep properly.

Exercise 6

Put in suitable adjectives.

1 Iron is not as _____ as lead.

2 How _____ of you to cross the road without looking first!

3 Wood is not as _____ a conductor of electricity as metals are.

4 Mary's toothache was so _____ that she went to a dentist.

5 A tropical storm is not as _____ or as _____ as a hurricane is.

6 How _____ you are now, Anne! You have grown several inches.

7 How _____ of you to help us yesterday! Thank you very much.

8 Sometimes the roads in town are so _____ with traffic that it is faster to walk.

5.6 Uses of adjectives (2)

a every + a singular noun + a singular verb

    1 Every student hopes to be successful in life.

    2 Not every country has a powerful army and air force.

b adjective + enough

    1 Are you old enough to enter the competition?

    2 John is not heavy enough to join our tug-of-war team.

c adjective + adjective

Sometimes we use the comparative form of an adjective in sentences like these:

    1 During the day, it becomes hotter and hotter but at night it becomes cooler and cooler.

    2 Between the ages of about 12 and 14, both boys and girls become taller and taller. They also become more and more intelligent.

    3 Land has become more and more expensive in the past ten years.

Exercise 7

Choose the right words from the brackets.

    1 Every (animal, animals) (need, needs) food and water to stay alive.

    2 Nearly every (pupil, pupils) in my class (know, knows) how to swim.

    3 Are you (enough young, young enough) to take part in the competition?

    4 Is the food (enough cool, cool enough) to eat yet?

    5 When you walk into the sea, the water becomes (wetter and wetter, deeper and deeper).

    6 House lizards are not (small, slow, big) enough to catch birds.

    7 It is true that every (country, countries) (export, exports) goods to other countries. If (they, it) (does, do) not do this, it cannot import goods.

    8 Are those shoes (deep, dry, big, cold) enough for you? Are they (suitable, comfortable) enough?

5.7 Adjective + a preposition

Check that you understand these expressions and can use them.

absent from a meeting	fit for us	qualified for promotion
according to Susan	fond of fruit	quick at her work
afraid of them	foolish of you	ready for the game
agree with us	free of charge	responsible to them
angry with him	full of curiosity	responsible for him
angry about it	generous of you	rude of him to say
annoyed with him	good at maths	safe from danger
annoyed about it	good for your health	safe for you to go
ashamed of himself	good of you to help	satisfied with it
astonished by it	grateful to her	selfish of him to say
aware of the danger	guilty of robbery	separate from others
bad at maths	hard for him to do	serious about the plan
bad for you	harmful to/for you	shocked at/by the news
brave of her	hopeless at maths	sick of waiting for him
busy writing	ignorant of the truth	similar to the others
busy with a friend	important for you to	sorry about the result
capable of doing it	inconvenient for us	south of the equator
careful with it	inferior to hers	stupid of them to say
certain of succeeding	interested in music	sufficient for us
clever with her hands	keen on helping	suitable for our work
clever at physics	kind of you to come	superior to others
close to the hotel	late for school	sure of winning
confident of winning	loyal to the manageress	surprised at that
convenient for us	lucky for you that	surprised by that
delighted with the news	married to Mary	suspicious of them
	necessary for us to	tired of waiting
different from you	new to me	uneasy about the plan
disappointed with them	obvious to everybody	
	patient with him	useful to us
disappointed by him	pleased with them	useful for repairing
disappointed at not - ing		

doubtful about the result	prejudiced against him	weak at English
		weak in English
essential for our plan	prepared for trouble	worried about them
excited about the game		worried by the news
expert at repairing	protected against it	wrong of him to say
familiar with the area	puzzled about them	
famous for its beauty	puzzled by his reply	

Exercise 8

Choose the letter of the best word to use each time.

1 I hope this visit is not inconvenient _____ you.

  A for   C with
  B at   D about

2 Is she capable_____ doing it _____ herself?

  A to ____ by C to ____ for
  B of ____ by D of ____ at

3 This coin is different _____ the other ones.

  A than   C with
  B to   D from

4 This machine is superior _____ those.

  A to   C by
  B than   D at

5 He felt ashamed _____ himself.

  A with   C of
  B to   D for

6 Do you agree _____ her?

  A to   C at
  B with   D on

7 There is sufficient food here _____ at least five people.

  A for   C with
  B to   D about

8 You'll have to be patient _____ her. This job is new to her.

  A at   C with
  B of   D by

9 It was rude _____ him to say that he was tired _____ waiting for us.

  A of ____ by C by ____ of
  B from ____ of D of ____ of

10 Tom: What happened at the trial?

  Sue: He pleaded not guilty, but he was found guilty _____ drunk driving.

  A to   C for
  B of   D with

5.8　Forming adjectives

Common adjective endings are shown below. Make adjectives with the same endings from the words in brackets.

-able:　inevitable, reliable (misery, charity, comfort, value)

-al:　　capital, immortal, feudal (nature, brute, season, accident)

-an:　　Jamaican, Indonesian (Europe, America, Mexico, India, Mauritius)

-ant:　　vacant, extravagant, abundant, elegant (brilliance, distance, ignorance)

-ar:　　similar, lunar, particular, regular (triangle, circle, spectacle, pole)

-ary:　　ordinary, temporary, necessary, contrary (custom, document, honour, legend)

-ate:　　separate, adequate, desolate, ultimate, accurate

-ed:　　increased, borrowed, cooked (boil, damage, fry, sharpen, smash, melt)

-en:　　sudden, written, beaten (drink, freeze, sink, gold, wood, break)

-ent:　　silent, absent, patient, frequent, confident (differ, excel, persist)

-ful:　　grateful, doubtful, merciful, delightful (thank, hope, help, use, care)

-ible:　　(im)possible, terrible, horrible, visible, edible (sense)

-ic:　　civic, democratic, pacific (acrobat, atom, cube, sympathy, drama)

-ical:　　tropical, poetical, identical, geographical (grammar, history, music)

-id:　　solid, vivid, timid, stupid, horrid, fluid, liquid, rapid, splendid

Exercise 9

Put one of the above adjectives on each line below so that you match each adjective with its meaning.

1 _____ showing a lot of mercy to somebody or something

2 _____ cannot be done; not possible at all

3 _____ from or living in Europe

4 _____ not speaking or making a noise

5 _____ fast or very fast

6 _____ (of water) heated until it begins to bubble

7 _____ in the shape of a triangle

8 _____ a long way away

9 _____ worth a lot of money

10 _____ occurring at certain times (of the year) only

-ing: growing, damaging, winning, working (break, test, wash, increase, change)

-ious: anxious, cautious, obvious, precious, glorious, conscious (mystery, vary)

-ish: yellowish, selfish, English, Jewish (baby, boy, child, fool, sheep)

-ive: descriptive, negative, positive, talkative (attract, act, explode, excess)

-less: senseless, voiceless, stainless, pointless (use, care, help, hope, end)

-like: warlike, childlike, lifelike, businesslike

-ly: jolly, shapely, curly, chilly, deadly (brother, cost, love, coward, friend)

-ory: satisfactory, compulsory, introductory, advisory

-ous: numerous, humorous, jealous, tremendous (poison, marvel, mischief, fame)

-uous: continuous, ambiguous, superfluous, virtuous, strenuous

-y: busy, dirty, wealthy, crazy, funny, greasy (anger, cloud, hunger, speed)

Exercise 10

Form adjectives from these words:

1 clock	6 science	11 mountain	16 steam	21 value
2 gold	7 artist	12 industry	17 skill	22 child
3 month	8 harm	13 poison	18 red	23 noise
4 history	9 home	14 danger	19 picture	24 expense
5 giant	10 victory	15 rust	20 enjoy	25 prime

6 Articles

6.1   Using 'a' and 'an'

a 'A' and 'an' mean 'a(any) one' but 'the' refers to a known person or thing. Compare these sentences.

   (i)   Can I have a cake?

   (ii) Can I have the cake on the table?

We often use 'a' or 'an' in these ways:

   • when we mean 'any one' and not a special one:

      Can you lend me a dollar?   Have you got a watch?

   • when we say a person's occupation:

      My mother is a teacher.   Mrs King is a nurse.

   • in some fixed expressions such as these:

      $10 a kilo   have a rest   make a mistake

      a lot of it   go for a swim in half an hour

b Use 'an' instead of 'a' when the next word starts with a silent 'h' or a vowel sound. There are more than fifteen vowel sounds. You can hear some of them when you say these words:

      That pen is not much good. (six vowel sounds)

      Pa, may we all go too?   (another six vowel sounds)

We call the letters a, e, i, o and u 'vowels' but they are not vowel sounds in some words. The spelling of a word does not always tell us whether to use 'an' instead of 'a'. We have to listen and see how the word is pronounced.

with 'an		with 'a'	
an axe	an 'f'	a sharp axe	a hotel
an egg	an hour	a European	a one-way street
an Indian	an 'm'	a ewe	a one-armed man
an orange	an X-ray	a union	
an umbrella	an S-bend	a Eurasian	a history book
		a 'u'	

Exercise 1

Put in 'a' or 'an'.

1 A male sheep is called _____ ram, and a female one is called _____ ewe.

2 You have left _____ 'u' out of this word and _____'r' out of that one.

3 Mr Oni is _____ honest man, so he will tell us if he makes _____ mistake.

4 _____ few years ago, _____ RAF plane landed on _____ small ship at sea.

5 The police have arrested _____ 18-year-old man as _____ result of information from _____ member of the public.

6 My sister goes to _____ university in America; my brother is _____ waiter in _____ hotel in the tourist district.

7 Our school is _____ L-shaped building. It is quite _____ old building.

8 Can you give me _____ example of a word containing three different vowels?

9 Yes, that's not much of _____ problem. As _____ matter of fact, I can think of several words.

10 What _____ horrible thing to say! Did he have _____ reason for saying that?

6.2   Using 'the'

We use 'the' to refer to a definite person or thing. Common uses include:

> • with a superlative:
>
> John is the oldest of the group but Kate is the tallest.
>
> • with people or things when there is one only
>
> the moon, the sun, the start, the end, the kitchen, the chairperson
>
> • before the name of a particular river, ocean, hotel, ship, newspapers, etc.
>
> the MV 'Ocean Star', the River Amazon, the Ritz hotel
>
> • before the names of some countries
>
> | | | |
> |---|---|---|
> | the Philippines | the UK | the Republic of ... |
> | the Argentine | the (former) USSR | the United Arab Republic |

We do NOT use 'the' before the names of most countries.

We do not usually need 'the' before a plural noun unless we add more words to show which group we are talking about. Compare these sentences:

(i)   Sometimes players argue with spectators.

(ii) One player argued with the spectators in the new stand.

6.3   No article needed

We do not need a, an or the with these words:

> • before the names of most countries:
>
>> in France, from Zimbabwe, to Jamaica, in
>> Thailand, from Singapore
>
> • before the names of lakes, islands and capes
>
>> on Lake Victoria, towards Penang Island,
>> round Cape Horn

But we use 'the' when we put 'island' first, e.g. the island of Penang.

> • with 'play' + a game
>
>> play tennis   play football
>> play billiards   play snooker
>
> • with 'have' + a meal (unless we refer to a specific
> meal)
>
>> Have you had lunch yet? What time did you
>>   have breakfast?
>
> • before the names of most festivals and holidays
>
>> It rained at Christmas and on New Year's day.
>
> • before gerunds and abstract nouns used in a
> general sense
>
>> Mary likes reading and talking to her friends.
>
>> Her success is due to hard work and not to luck.
>
> • before uncountable nouns
>
>> That tin is full of sugar or rice.

Exercise 2

Choose the best answer each time. XXX means that no article is needed.

1 Can you tell us ... quickest way to ... nearest police station?

A the _____ XXX   C XXX _____ XXX
B XXX _____ the   D the _____ the

2 _____ international film company wants to hire _____ small island to make a film on.

A An _____ XXX   C The _____ an
B An _____ a   D The _____ XXX

3 My friend has _____ old-fashioned piano in _____ living-room of her home.

A the _____ the   C an _____ the
B a _____ the   D an _____ XXX

4 The monitor of _____ class should set _____ good example to other pupils.

A the _____ XXX   C XXX _____ the
B a _____ an   D a _____ a

5 Sometimes it is difficult for _____ motorists to find _____ place to park.

A XXX _____ a   C XXX _____ XXX
B the _____ the   D the _____ XXX

6 If you want to reach _____ Silver Island, you must get on _____ ferry.

A XXX _____ a   C the _____ XXX
B XXX _____ XXX   D the _____ a

7 Hong Kong is _____ well-known port in _____ Far East.

A the _____ XXX   C a _____ the
B a _____ XXX   D XXX _____ the

7 Verbs (I)

1 Finite and non-finite verbs	*4* Main and auxiliary verbs
2 The structure of sentences	*5* Active and passive verb forms
3 Agreement of verb and subject	*6* The principal parts of verbs

In this chapter, you can learn about verbs. The information in the chapter will help you to avoid making mistakes, so study each section carefully.

7.1 Finite and non-finite verbs

We saw in 2.6 that verbs express an action or make a statement about a person or thing.

> Mary gave her sister a present.
> Susan was very pleased. She thanked Mary.

A finite verb is a 'working' verb with a subject; it can be in any tense.

A non-finite (or infinite) verb has no subject and is not in any tense. It can be:

an infinitive:	(to) walk	(to) be	(to) be arrested
a present participle:	walking	being	being arrested
a past participle:	walked	been	arrested

We must use at least one subject and finite verb in each sentence. Compare the following:

a sentence:	I could not sleep because of the noise made by the traffic.
NOT a sentence:	Because of the noise made by the traffic.
a sentence:	We heard two spectators arguing about the game.
NOT a sentence:	Arguing about the game.
a sentence:	My mother went to the market to buy some meat and vegetables.
NOT a sentence:	To buy some meat and vegetables.

Exercise 1

Are the following sentences or not?

1 Walking very slowly across the road and trying to avoid the cars, buses and other traffic.

2 I saw an old woman walking quickly across the road.

3 Scolded for losing his money.

4 Kanu was scolded for losing his money on his way home.

5 To save up as much money as possible.

6 Struck by lightning during a severe storm yesterday afternoon.

7 It is wise to save up as much money as you can.

8 A tree was struck by lightning during a storm yesterday.

9 In the kitchen, helping her mother to prepare food for her sister's birthday party later on during the day.

10 Susan is helping her mother to prepare food for the birthday party.

7.2 The structure of sentences

Study the way in which we can make a sentence longer by adding information about a person, a thing or an action.

Step 1 My brother found a wallet.

Step 2 My brother, who is often very lucky, found a wallet.

Step 3 My brother, who is often very lucky, found a wallet which contained a large sum of money.

Step 4 My brother, who is often very lucky, found a wallet which contained a large sum of money when he was walking home.

Step 5 My brother, who is often very lucky, found a wallet which contained a large sum of money when he was walking home, so he took it to a police station not far away.

All the above sentences are correct. We cannot break any of the sentences into two parts and make two 'sentences'. The following expressions are NOT sentences by themselves:

a who is often very lucky

b which contained a large sum of money

c when he was walking home

d so he took it to a police station not far away

The statements in (a) to (d) do not make complete sense by themselves, so they are not sentences.

Exercise 2

Correct the following by changing them into complete sentences.

1 We watched a film on television. About how bears catch fish in a river.

2 Mary turned off the light. Not realising that her father was asleep in a chair.

3 Yesterday John helped his father. To repair a leaking tap at home.

4 Susan was delighted. When the manager offered her a job in the office.

5 The fishermen turned round and headed for the harbour. When they saw black clouds appear in the east.

6 John repaired his bicycle. So that he could go for a ride with his friends.

7 Mrs King complained to the manager of the shop. Because her new watch stopped two days after she had bought it.

8 Put the tools back in their right places. If you have finished with them.

7.3   Agreement of verb and subject

a   The verb must agree with its subject in a sentence, e.g.

is/are	*1* My friend is late. My friends are late.
was/were	*2* Somebody was hurt. Four people were hurt.
has/have	*3* Susan has a cold. Her friends have a cold.
does/do	*4* Does he live here? Do they live here?
S. Present	*5* My father likes coffee. My parents like coffee.
that/those	*6* That book is yours. Those books are Mary's.
this/these	*7* This box is fine. These boxes are too big.

b Check that you understand these points:

there/here/where is/are   In expressions such as 'There are the girls', the subject (girls) comes after the verb. Make sure that your verb agrees with the following subject.

1 Here is the key to the cupboard.

2 Here are the keys you want.

3 There is a woman in the back of the car.

4 There are two children in the back of the car.

every   After 'every' we use a singular noun and verb.

5 Every country has an army.

6 Every person needs water, food and a home.

none   It is correct to use a singular OR a plural verb with 'none'. You can please yourself whether your verb is singular or plural.

7 None of the girls are ready.

8 None of the girls is ready.

a lot of   Use a plural verb when 'a lot of' refers to a plural countable noun.

Use a singular verb when it refers to a singular uncountable noun.

9 A lot of these bananas are bad.

10 A lot of this meat is bad.

one of the ...   We use a singular verb with 'one of the
more than one ...   ...' and with 'more than one ...' (although it has a plural meaning).

11 One of the players is John's cousin.

12 There IS more than one way of solving the problem.

the ... of the ...   In this expression, the subject is the first noun and the verb agrees with it. Study these sentences:

13 The results of the test WERE a surprise.

14 The decision of the judges WAS a surprise.

Be careful when the verb is a long way from its subject:

15 The result of the inquiry in which experts investigated the causes of the fires WAS extremely interesting.

16 The evidence of nearly all the eye-witnesses who saw the lorry hit two cars SHOWS that the lorry-driver was to blame.

Exercise 3

Put in 'is' or 'are'.

1 Where _____ the key to this door?

2 Who _____ those two women?

3 _____ all the meat bad?

4 _____ all the girls here?

5 Those _____ Ann's shoes.

6 That _____ Uncle's new car.

7 There _____ nobody in it.

8 Where _____ your friends?

9 Everybody _____ ready now.

10 None of them _____ absent.

11 There _____ a number of boys absent.

12 More than one island _____ popular with tourists.

13 The car by those trees _____ my father's.

14 Everything _____ ready for the party.

15 A lot of this maize _____ bad.

16 There _____ not a lot of bananas left.

17 All that information _____ correct.

18 All the news _____ good today.

19 Here _____ the stamps you wanted.

20 This pair _____ too expensive.

Exercise 4

Put in like or likes.

1 Every girl _____ pretty clothes.

2 No policeman _____ thieves.

3 We both _____ pineapples.

4 Some of them _____ papayas.

5 Does she _____ coffee?

6 None of the boys _____ black coffee.

7 One of the women _____ fried rice.

8 My best friend _____ swimming.

9 He _____ to sleep in the afternoon.

10 Nobody _____ to be blamed for a mistake.

7.4 Main and auxiliary verbs

In a and b below, the main verbs are underlined.

a The cars stopped at the traffic lights.

b I think the last bus leaves at ten thirty.

Auxiliary (helping) verbs are used to make tenses, questions, negatives and short replies. In c, d and e, the auxiliary verbs are underlined.

c The lorry did not stop at the lights, so there was an accident.

d Have you seen Ramli recently?

e Mary: John likes to play table-tennis.

Sue: So does Peter.

Exercise 5

Choose the right words from the brackets.

1 John collects stamps and so (do, does) his brother.

2 You can go out when you (are, have) finished your work.

3 That bus doesn't go to the city and neither (is, does) that one.

4 Hello, John. What (are, will) you doing this evening?

5 (Will, Shall) we go fishing later on?

6 Mary has gone to the cinema and so (has, have) John and Peter.

7 (Has, Did) anybody phone while we were out?

8 Every week large quantities of oil (is, are) exported from the Middle East to Europe and other places.

7.5 Active and passive verb forms

When a verb is active, the subject does the action:
active verbs

a The policemen arrested two robbers and took them away.

b We congratulated Mary when she passed her driving test.

When a verb is passive, the action is done TO the subject:
passive verbs

c Two robbers were arrested and then they were taken away.

d Mary was congratulated by her friends.

7.6 The principal parts of verbs

Check that you know the following verbs:
In the following lists,

a the infinitive of the verb (without 'to')

b The Simple Past tense

c the Past Participle

/ / shows the sound made by the final -ed when we say it

(a)	(b) and (c)		(a)	(b) and (c)	
add	added	/id/	close	closed	/d/
advise	advised	/d/	collapse	collapsed	/t/
agree	agreed	/d/	collect	collected	/id/
allow	allowed	/d/	comb	combed	/d/
answer	answered	/d/	compare	compared	/d/
appear	appeared	/d/	complain	complained	/d/
apply	applied	/d/	complete	completed	/id/
arrange	arranged	/d/	continue	continued	/d/
arrest	arrested	/id/	cook	cooked	/t/
arrive	arrived	/d/	copy	copied	/id/
ask	asked	/t/	correct	corrected	/id/
attack	attacked	/t/	cough	coughed	/t/
bark	barked	/t/	count	counted	/id/
behave	behaved	/d/	cover	covered	/d/
believe	believed	/d/	crash	crashed	/t/
belong	belonged	/d/	crawl	crawled	/d/
boil	boiled	/d/	cross	crossed	/t/
borrow	borrowed	/d/	cry	cried	/d/
breathe	breathed	/d/	damage	damaged	/d/
bury	buried	/id/	dance	danced	/t/
call	called	/d/	decide	decided	/id/
care	cared	/d/	decorate	decorated	/id/
carry	carried	/id/	decrease	decreased	/t/
cause	caused	/d/	defeat	defeated	/id/
change	changed	/d/	defend	defended	/id/
chase	chased	/t/	deliver	delivered	/d/
cheat	cheated	/id/	demand	demanded	/id/
check	checked	/t/	describe	described	/d/
cheer	cheered	/d/	destroy	destroyed	/d/
clap	clapped	/t/	detect	detected	/id/
clean	cleaned	/d/	die	died	/d/
climb	climbed	/d/	dip	dipped	/t/

(a)	(b) and (c)		(a)	(b) and (c)	
direct	directed	/id/	help	helped	/t/
disappear	disappeared	/d/	hope	hoped	/t/
dislike	disliked	/t/	hurry	hurried	/id/
divide	divided	/id/	improve	improved	/d/
dress	dressed	/t/	increase	increased	/t/
drop	dropped	/t/	invite	invited	/id/
drown	drowned	/d/	join	joined	/d/
dry	dried	/d/	jump	jumped	/t/
enclose	enclosed	/d/	kick	kicked	/t/
enjoy	enjoyed	/d/	laugh	laughed	/t/
enter	entered	/d/	lift	lifted	/id/
escape	escaped	/t/	like	liked	/t/
expect	expected	/id/	listen	listened	/d/
explore	explored	/d/	live	lived	/d/
fail	failed	/d/	look	looked	/t/
fasten	fastened	/d/	love	loved	/d/
finish	finished	/t/	manage	managed	/d/
fish	fished	/t/	march	marched	/t/
fit	fitted	/id	mark	marked	/t/
float	floated	/id/	marry	married	/id/
flow	flowed	/d/	measure	measured	/d/
fold	folded	/id/	melt	melted	/id/
follow	followed	/d/	mend	mended	/id/
frighten	frightened	/d/	move	moved	/d/
fry	fried	/d/	nail	nailed	/d/
glue	glued	/d/	notice	noticed	/t/
guess	guessed	/t/	obey	obeyed	/d/
guide	guided	/id/	obtain	obtained	/d/
hand	handed	/id/	offer	offered	/d/
happen	happened	/d/	open	opened	/d/
hate	hated	/id/	order	ordered	/d/
heat	heated	/id/	paint	painted	/id/

(a)	(b) and (c)		(a)	(b) and (c)	
pass	passed	/t/	reply	replied	/d/
peel	peeled	/d/	rescue	rescued	/d/
pick	picked	/t/	return	returned	/d/
pin	pinned	/d/	roamed	roamed	/d/
place	placed	/t/	roar	roared	/d/
plan	planned	/d/	rob	robbed	/d/
plant	planted	/id/	roll	rolled	/d/
play	played	/d/	row	rowed	/d/
please	pleased	/d/	rub	rubbed	/d/
point	pointed	/id/	rule	ruled	/d/
poke	poked	/t/	rush	rushed	/t/
polish	polished	/t/	sail	sailed	/d/
possess	possessed	/t/	save	saved	/d/
practise	practised	/t/	score	scored	/d/
pray	prayed	/d/	search	searched	/t/
prefer	preferred	/d/	seize	seized	/d/
prepare	prepared	/d/	serve	served	/d/
press	pressed	/t/	shape	shaped	/t/
pretend	pretended	/id/	share	shared	/d/
print	printed	/id/	sharpen	sharpened	/d/
prove	proved	/d/	shout	shouted	/id/
provide	provided	/id/	show	showed	/d/
pull	pulled	/d/	slip	slipped	/t/
push	pushed	/t/	slow	slowed	/d/
rain	rained	/d/	smash	smashed	/t/
raise	raised	/d/	splash	splashed	/t/
reach	reached	/t/	squeeze	squeezed	/d/
receive	received	/d/	stare	stared	/d/
reduce	reduced	/t/	start	started	/id/
remove	removed	/d/	stay	stayed	/d/
repair	repaired	/d/	stir	stirred	/d/
repeat	repeated	/id/	stop	stopped	/t/

(a)	(b) and (c)		(a)	(b) and (c)	
stretch	stretched	/t/	wait	waited	/id/
study	studied	/id/	walk	walked	/t/
switch	switched	/t/	want	wanted	/id/
talk	talked	/t/	warn	warned	/d/
tap	tapped	/t/	wash	washed	/t/
telephone	telephoned	/d/	watch	watched	/t/
test	tested	/id/	water	watered	/d/
thank	thanked	/t/	wave	waved	/d/
threaten	threatened	/d/	weigh	weighed	/d/
tie	tied	/d/	whip	whipped	/t/
touch	touched	/t/	whisper	whispered	/d/
trap	trapped	/t/	wipe	wiped	/t/
travel	travelled	/d/	wish	wished	/t/
try	tried	/d/	wonder	wondered	/d/
turn	turned	/d/	work	worked	/t/
type	typed	/t/	worry	worried	/id/
use	used	/d/	wound	wounded	/id/
visit	visited	/id/	wrap	wrapped	/t/

Some verbs have the same form for the infinitive, past tense and past participle.
They include these verbs:

bet	cast	cut	hit	shed
let	broadcast	shut	slit	spread
set	forecast	put	split	hurt
upset	cost	thrust	rid	

The following verbs have the same form for their Simple Past tense and their past participle.

(a)	(b) and (c)	(a)	(b) and (c)
bend	bent	light	lit/lighted
bind	bound	make	made
bleed	bled	mean	meant
bring	brought	meet	met
build	built	pay	paid
burn	burnt	read	read
buy	bought	say	said
catch	caught	sell	sold
creep	crept	send	sent
deal	dealt	shine	shone
dig	dug	shoot	shot
dwell	dwelt	sit	sat
feed	fed	sleep	slept
feel	felt	slide	slid
fight	fought	spend	spent
find	found	spill	spilt
get	got	stand	stood
have	had	stick	stuck
hear	heard	strike	struck
hold	held	sweep	swept
keep	kept	teach	taught
kneel	knelt	tell	told
lead	led	think	thought
learn	learnt	understand	understood
leave	left	win	won
lend	lent	wind	wound

These verbs are more difficult. Check that you know how to use them. Reminder:

a the infinitive *b* the Simple Past form *c* the past participle

(a)	(b)	(c)	(a)	(b)	(c)
be	was	been	hide	hid	hidden
beat	beat	beaten	know	knew	known
become	became	become	ride	rode	ridden
begin	began	begun	ring	rang	rung
bite	bit	bitten	rise	rose	risen
blow	blew	blown	run	ran	run
break	broke	broken	see	saw	seen
choose	chose	chosen	shake	shook	shaken
come	came	come	show	showed	shown
do	did	done	sing	sang	sung
draw	drew	drawn	sink	sank	sunk
drink	drank	drunk	speak	spoke	spoken
drive	drove	driven	steal	stole	stolen
eat	ate	eaten	swim	swam	swum
fall	fell	fallen	take	took	taken
fly	flew	flown	tear	tore	torn
forget	forgot	forgotten	throw	threw	thrown
freeze	froze	frozen	wake	woke	woken
go	went	gone	wear	wore	worn
grow	grew	grown	write	wrote	written

The past participles in column (c) are used to make these tenses:

1 The Present Perfect tense with has or have:

    a What have you broken?

    b Has Mary spoken to you about the party yet?

2 The Past Perfect tense with had:

    a John told us that he had not seen Michael for several weeks.

    b Susan felt tired after she had swum for nearly an hour.

3 The passive form of all tenses:

   a We can't use our car because it is being repaired now.

   b My cousin's bicycle was stolen during the night.

   c Every day somebody is arrested for breaking the law.

   d The escaped prisoners will soon be caught.

   e Your old shoes have been thrown away.

Exercise 6

Put in the right form of the verbs in brackets.

1 I have (forget) my keys.

2 Have you (write) to Tom yet?

3 Did you (go) swimming?

4 We (go) for a walk last night.

5 Yesterday I (write) to Susan.

6 Somebody has (take) my pen.

7 Ow! I've (bite) my tongue.

8 How much have you (lose)?

9 Have the police (catch) the men?

10 The warning was (broadcast) on the radio a few days ago.

11 Did you (understand) what he said?

12 We (grow) tomatoes last year.

13 Have you (speak) to Ann yet?

14 You (play) well yesterday.

15 The birds (fly) away when I came out.

16 When did you (draw) that picture?

17 Mary (sing) well last night.

18 Has the manager (pay) you yet?

19 I've just (find) some money.

20 The man asked us if anybody had been (hurt) in the accident.

Exercise 7

The following things have just happened. Put in the past participle of the verbs in brackets.

1 A ship has (sink).

2 Ten men have been (rescue).

3 A lot of oil has been (spill).

4 Some fish have been (kill).

5 The oil has (catch) fire.

6 A radio message has been (send).

7 A helicopter has (arrive).

8 The pilot has (see) men in the water.

9 A ship has been (ask) to help.

10 Two lifeboats have been (launch).

8 Verbs (2): Tenses

1 Simple Present tense	*5* Present Perfect tense
2 Present Continuous tense	*6* Past Perfect tense
3 Past Continuous tense	*7* Simple Future tense
4 Simple Past tense	

The aim of this chapter is to give you a chance to review the use of the main tenses in English.

8.1 Simple Present tense

Forms: *a* I like   he/she/it likes

       b I do like   he does like

We use b for emphasis and in questions and negative statements.
Make sure that in (a) you add an 's' if the subject is he, she, it or a noun which could replace them.

Uses: (i)   The main use is for present actions which are habits.

         My friend lives near me and always walks to school.

  (ii) This tense can be used for regular travel arrangements.

         Uncle leaves for New York next Monday.

  (iii) This tense is often used in newspaper headlines about past actions.

         GOVERNMENT RAISES TAX ON PETROL

             UN AGREES SANCTIONS

  (iv) This tense can be used instead of the S. Future tense after 'when', 'before', 'after' and 'if' when we refer to the future.

         We'll have a big dinner if Uncle comes next Saturday.

         Give this to Mary when you see her tomorrow.

8.2 Present Continuous tense

Forms: am/is/are (not) + a present participle

Mary is waiting. It is raining. The girls are coming.

Uses: (i) The main use is for temporary action which is happening at the time of speaking but which will finish (soon).

It is raining heavily at the minute.

Father is watching a film on television.

(ii) This tense can be used for planned future actions, especially ones involving movement.

Q: What are you doing on Saturday?

A: I'm going swimming with some friends.

Exercise 1

Put in the correct present forms of the verbs in brackets.

1 John (study) in Form 2 now. That is Grade 8.

2 That small island (belong) to a private company.

3 How people (spend) their leisure (depend) on how old they are.

4 Follow this path. It (lead) to the river. You'll see Mr Young's house when you (reach) the river.

5 Tell Mary to be careful. The boat may tip up if she (stand) up in it.

6 How many guests (come) to Mary's party on Saturday? Is it true that John (come)?

7 Please take a message if anybody (phone) while we're out.

8 Shall I tell Ann about the meeting? I (meet) her tomorrow morning.

9 My uncle and aunt (come) to see us next Saturday evening.

10 Listen! I think two women (come) up the stairs. I think they (argue) about something.

8.3 Past Continuous tense

Forms: was/were + a present participle

Q: What were you doing at 8.30 last night?

A: I was writing a letter at home.

Uses: (i) The main use of this tense is to show what was happening at a past time, as in the examples on p.64.

(ii) This tense replaces the Present Continuous tense in Reported Speech.

She told us she was going to the beach this evening.

(iii) We can also use this tense for a cancelled future action.

I was going to buy a new radio but now I can't afford one.

8.4 Simple Past tense

Forms: *a* The bus stopped.

b The bus did stop.

We use (**b**) for emphasis and in questions and negative statements.

Uses: (i) The main use is for completed past actions when the time is known or stated. (If the time is not known we can often use the Present Perfect tense instead.)

(ii) We also use the Simple Past tense in conditional clauses when we make a general statement or speak about an unlikely event.

If motorists drove more carefully, there would be fewer accidents.

(iii) The Simple Past tense can be used for habitual past actions.

My mother often played hockey when she was younger.

(iv) It is used after 'I wish' and 'If only' when referring to present time.

I wish we lived nearer a big city.

If only Mother and Father were here now!

(v) We also use the Simple Past tense in these sentences:

Hurry up! It's time we left for the station.

Nine o'clock! It's time I went home.

I would rather you didn't tell anybody about the mistake.

Mary would rather we didn't invite Susan again.

8.5 Present Perfect tense

Forms: has/have + a past participle

> Mother has just gone to speak to Mrs Lee.

> Can I go out now? I've finished all my homework.

Uses: (i) The main use of this tense is with already, just, now and recently in statements and ever in questions when we speak about a recently completed action.

(ii) We can use this tense for any past action when we do not state or know the time of the action. Do NOT use this tense if you state the time of the action.

wrong: Thank you for your letter which I have received this morning.

right: Thank you for your letter which I received this morning.

Exercise 2

Study each situation. Then put in the Simple Past or Present Perfect forms of the verbs in brackets.

1 Last night a tree (fall) down and (block) the road near our house. Some workmen (just come) to cut the tree up and take it away.

2 Mary is out. She (go) to see a neighbour a few minutes ago.

3 Many years ago, dangerous wild animals (live) in that forest but in recent years people (cut) down the trees and the animals (disappear).

4 I'm hungry. It's time we (have) lunch. Shall we go to a restaurant?

5 No, thanks. I'd rather we (stay) here and (have) lunch at home.

6 (see) you Peter recently?

7 Yes, I (see) him at the market last Saturday.

8 Put your books away if you (finish) with them.

9 Look at the time! It's nearly midnight. It's time we (go) to bed.

10 This is the first time I (play) badminton, so I expect I'll make many mistakes.

8.6   Past Perfect tense

Form: had + a past participle

> When we reached John's house, we found that he had already gone out.

> I wish you hadn't told Peter about the party.

Uses: (i)   The main use of this tense is to show which of two past actions happened first.

> Mary suddenly remembered that she had left her keys at home.

> We stopped for a rest after we had walked about four miles.

(ii) This tense is also used in reported speech:

> Mary told us that she had just passed her driving test.

(iii) The Past Perfect tense is also used in conditional sentences which refer to the past.

> If you had told me that you had no money, we would have lent you some.

> The other car would have hit us if Uncle hadn't swerved suddenly.

(iv) It is used after I wish, if only, I would rather and I would sooner when we refer to a past event.

> I wish I hadn't spent all my money!

> If only Father had been here! He would have helped us.

> I would rather you hadn't lent him so much money.

Exercise 3

Decide which action in each sentence happened first. Put in the Past Perfect form of one verb, and the Simple Past form of the other verb.

1 The policeman (want) to know who (phone) 999.

2 Mary (admit) that she (make) the phone call.

3 She (say) that they (see) somebody breaking into a neighbour's home.

4 When the police arrived at the neighbour's house, they (notice) that somebody (break) into the house through a window.

5 'The burglar (smash) a window before we (arrive),' the police sergeant said.

6 When the neighbours came home, they (discover) that somebody (take) money and jewellery from their home.

7 They (nail) wooden planks across the window which the burglar (use) to get in.

8 Then they (start) to tidy up the mess which the burglar (cause).

9 The policeman (ask) them if they (report) the burglary to their insurance company.

10 'The jewellery wasn't insured,' Mr King said. 'If we (know) that there (be) so much crime in the area, we would have insured it.'

8.7 The Simple Future tense

Form: shall/will + an infinitive without 'to'

Do you think our team will win on Saturday?

Shall I close the windows now?

In questions we use 'shall' before 'I' and 'we'. In most statements, it does not matter whether we use 'shall' or 'will' after 'I' and 'we'.

We will arrive at about half past ten.

We shall arrive at about half past ten.

Use: The main use of the Simple Future tense is for planned or unplanned future events.

planned: Uncle's plane will arrive at three o'clock.

unplanned: Who will win the 100 metres race?

We often use 'Shall' to start a suggestion. Then it can mean 'Do you want (to do something)' or 'Would you like me (to do something)'.

Shall we go swimming this evening?

It's getting dark. Shall I turn on the light?

Exercise 4

Choose the best word(s) each time.

1 What _____ you _____ if you win the lottery?

  A have _____   C are _____
     done   doing
  B will _____   D did _____
     do   do

2 Where _____ John _____ when he comes?

  A has _____   C will _____
     stayed   stay
  B do _____   D is _____
     stay   stayed

3 How many eggs _____ you _____?

  A are _____   C have _____
     wanting   wanted
  B shall _____   D do _____
     want   want

4 What time _____ the game finish?

  A is   C has
  B does   D do

5 We _____ a big crab on the beach.

  A seen   C see
  B saw   D seeing

6 Did you _____ this jug?

  A break   C broken
  B broke   D breaking

7 We _____ no money, so we did not _____ to the cinema.

  A had _____   C have _____
     go   went
  B having _____   D has _____
     went   go

8 The driver denied that he _____ the accident by driving carelessly.

  A had caused   C was caused
  B has caused   D cause

9 We would have lost the game if John _____ played for us.

  A isn't   C cannot
  B haven't   D hadn't

10 Mary is absent. She _____ a bad cold.

  A having   C has
  B is having   D have

11 She lives here but _____ in the city.

  A working   C have
                      worked
  B work   D works

12 Shall we ... to Mary's house?

  A went   C going
  B gone   D go

9   Infinitives

9.1   What is an infinitive?

It is the root or base of a verb before we add any endings to it. We can use an infinitive with or without 'to':

a My brother likes to collect stamps. You can collect them too if you like.

b Mrs King went to the market to buy some vegetables and fish.

c We must post these letters when we go out.

9.2   Forms of the infinitive

Forms of the infinitive include the ones shown below. We omit 'to' after such words as can, could, may, might and must.

Present

active	(to) arrest	(to) throw away
passive	(to) be arrested	(to) be thrown away

Perfect

active	(to) have arrested	(to) have thrown away
passive	(to) have been arrested	(to) have been thrown away

Examples in the same order as above:

1 Policemen ought to arrest drunk drivers.

2 All drunk drivers should be arrested.

3 The police sergeant ought to have arrested the guilty driver.

4 The driver killed a child, so he should have been arrested.

Exercise 1

Put in suitable infinitives. The sentences show some of the ways in which we use infinitives.

1 My mother told me _____ up my clothes and _____ them away neatly.

2 Susan went to the Post Office _____ some stamps and _____ some letters.

3 It is not easy _____ a word processor when it goes wrong.

4 Sometimes it is difficult _____ a bus between 7 a.m. and 8.30 a.m.

5 We saw that the road ahead of us was blocked by an accident. There was nothing left for us _____ except _____ round and go back the way we had come.

6 Three men have escaped from prison but they are certain _____ soon and taken back to prison.

7 When you want to cook fish, the first thing _____ is _____ the fish under a tap.

8 Sorry, I can't stop now. I'm on my way _____ my dentist.

9 Do you know how _____ a puncture in a tyre?

10 Yes. I'll show you how _____ it.

Exercise 2

Choose the best word(s) each time.

1 Haven't you finished yet? You ought _____ at least half an hour ago.

A to finish C to have finished
B be finished D have been finished

2 There is an old saying that children should _____ and not _____

A be seen _____ heard
B see _____ to be heard
C be seeing _____ be hearing
D have been seen _____ have been heard

3 What a nuisance! The traffic lights are still out of order. They ought _____ several days ago.

A to have been repaired
B to have repaired
C to have been repairing
D be repaired

4 This food is too hot _____

A to eat
B be eaten
C to eating
D to have eaten

5 Susan can't decide what dress _____ to the party this evening.

A wear
B wearing
C worn
D to wear

6 This road is too narrow. It ought _____

A widen
B widened
C be widened
D to be widened

7 Father wants to know where _____ his car.

A to park
B to parked
C to be parked
D have parked

8 Some men have been working on this road for nearly a month. These holes should _____ in before now.

A to have been filled
B filled
C have been filled
D be filling

9 It's hot. Would you like something _____ ?

A to be drunk   C to drink
B drink   D drunk

10 Those old shoes are no good now. They should _____ away.

A throw   C be throwing
B throwing   D be thrown

11 Uncle is late. He must _____ by the heavy traffic.

A delay
B have delayed
C have been delayed
D be delaying

12 Hurry! We must go and help the people in the car. Somebody may _____

A have been injured
B have injured
C to be injured
D to injure

10 Participles

10.1 Types of participles

These are common types of participles:

verb	present participle	past participle	perfect participle
wait	waiting	waited	having waited
break	breaking	broken	having broken
damage	damaging	damaged	having damaged

Exercise 1

Write out the present, past and perfect participles for the following verbs.

bite, draw, meet, buy, lose, write, steal, speak, hear, drive.

10.2 Using participles

a We can use many participles as adjectives, e.g.

a damaged car   a passing motorist   a threatening attitude

a broken window   an improved result   a wounded soldier

b A participle can start an expression in these ways:

present participles

(i) There is somebody waiting to see you.

(ii) Realising that she had forgotten her keys, Mary went back to get them.

(iii) Peter crawled through the barbed-wire, tearing his shirt as he did so.

When you use this type of expression, make sure that your sentence has only one meaning. Sentence (iv) is bad because it has two meanings. What are the two meanings and how could we change the sentence to give it only one meaning?

(iv) Looking out of a window, Peter saw a strange man.

past participles

(i) Terrified by the flood rushing towards them, the people tried to climb up trees to escape from the water.

(ii) The evidence discovered by the police helped to convict the guilty man.

(iii) The vehicle damaged in the accident has been towed away.

perfect participles

(i) Having missed the last bus, we had to walk home.

(ii) Never having visited St Lucia before, we were surprised to see how beautiful it is.

(iii) The girls finally managed to get tickets to the show, having waited nearly an hour.

Exercise 2

Use the information in each pair of sentences to make one sentence, using a present, past or perfect participle.

1 Mary spoke to the lady. The lady was sitting in the car.

2 We stopped to watch some men. They were repairing a burst water pipe.

3 John noticed some boys. They were fishing in the harbour.

4 Miss King was astonished at her good luck. She wondered what to do with the money.

5 We had not been to Nairobi before. We were surprised to see how modern it is.

6 Columbus was very pleased with himself. He thought he had found a new route to China and India.

7 Susan opened an envelope attached to the flowers. She wondered who could have sent them to her.

8 Mr Lee missed the last train. He had to travel by express bus.

9 Miss Menon switched on the television set. She intended to watch the news.

10 Ann put all her books away. She had finished her homework.

11 The men heard that gold had been discovered in the hills. They decided to give up their jobs and search for gold.

11 Adverbs

1 Understanding adverbs	*4* Forming adverbs
2 Adverb or adjective?	*5* Adverbial expressions (1)
3 Making comparisons	*6* Adverbial expressions (2)

11.1 Understanding adverbs

We saw in 2.7 that adverbs often show how, when or where an action takes place.

> how   Miss Johnson spoke quietly.

> when   There was a fire near our school yesterday.

> where There was a fire here.

When we use several adverbs or adverb expressions in one sentence, the order is often MANNER, PLACE, TIME (but we can change this to emphasize a word).

> The girls waited patiently at the bus stop for half an hour.
>   (manner)   (place)   (time)

Adverbs can also add information to an adjective or another adverb:

adv + adj
very tall
extremely cheap
rather angry.

adv + adv
very quietly
extremely carefully
slightly carelessly

11.2 Adverb or adjective?

It is a common mistake to use an adjective when an adverb is needed.

> wrong: She sang good.   right: She sang well.

> wrong: He smiled happy.   right: He smiled happily.

Exercise 1

Choose the right words from the brackets.

1 Ann lost all her money. (Lucky, Luckily) for her, a friend lent her enough money to get home (safe, safely).

2 We must look (deeper, more deeply) into the cause of the fire.

3 Please check these bills as (careful, carefully) as possible.

4 My friend can't speak English as (fluent, fluently) as he speaks Hindi.

5 Sometimes there are so many vehicles that they cause (serious, seriously) traffic jams.

6 You can float (more easily, easier) if you are not wearing heavy clothes and shoes.

7 My grandmother is always very (kind, kindly) to us.

8 Leela has passed her driving test (successful, successfully).

9 Try to make your work (more neatly, neater) by writing as (neat, neatly) as you can.

10 Mary took part in the competition (successful, successfully) and felt very (grateful, gratefully) to everybody who had helped her.

11.3 Making comparisons

We can make comparisons with adverbs in these ways:

Positive (one only)	Comparative (one of two only)	Superlative (one of three or more)
hard	harder	hardest
fast	faster	fastest
quickly	more quickly	most quickly
happily	more happily	most happily
well	better	best
badly	worse	worst

11.4 Forming adverbs

Many adverbs end in -ly but some do not. Some adjectives also end in -ly, e.g. curly, ugly, friendly, lovely and early. Examples of adverbs include these:

-ly   clearly, briefly, bravely, recently, loudly, usually, truly, weekly

-ily   sleepily, readily, hastily, noisily, unhappily, temporarily

-fully   cheerfully, hopefully, faithfully, carefully, gratefully

-ward(s)   backward(s), forward(s), eastward(s), northward(s), southward(s)

Exercise 2

Make adverbs from these words:

1 successful	*4* prompt	*7* lazy	*10* history	*13* fortunate
2 regular	*5* rapid	*8* greedy	*11* method	*14* second
3 lucky	*6* tidy	*9* cautious	*12* silent	*15* true

Exercise 3

In each line, which adverbs can we normally use with the given verb?

1 she spoke   quietly, angrily, stealthily, gracefully, simply, cheerfully

2 he boxed   skilfully, cleverly, prettily, noisily, carelessly, well

3 the bus came eventually, soon, immediately, accidentally, gratefully

4 she drove   well, badly, dangerously, cautiously, fast, slowly, brutally

5 Ann writes   sensibly, heroically, mentally, carefully, neatly, beautifully

6 he slept   soundly, happily, restlessly, rapidly, proudly, angrily, fitfully

7 we waited   patiently, impatiently, reluctantly, drunkenly, loudly, well

8 she ran   unsteadily, hurriedly, awkwardly, gracefully, cruelly

9 he smiled   grimly, nervously, cheerfully, happily, softly, loudly

10 it stopped   abruptly, suddenly, smoothly, normally, sweetly, loyally

Exercise 4

Complete each sentence by adding a suitable adverb.

1 We waited _____ for a bus to come.

2 Mr King woke up in the middle of the night when he heard a strange noise. He listened _____ and then lay down again.

3 Miss Lee opened the envelope _____ to see if there was a bill in it.

4 The dog barked _____ when a stranger approached the door.

5 Make sure that the rope is fastened _____ to the jetty. We don't want the boat to drift away.

6 If a cat sees a bird, it will approach _____ in an attempt to catch the bird.

7 A workman was _____ injured in an accident on a construction site yesterday. His funeral will be on Saturday.

8 Our cat defended its kittens _____ when a dog approached.

9 Mrs Young studied the agreement _____ before signing it.

10 The soldiers saluted _____ when their commander approached them.

11.5 Adverbial expressions (1)

Check that you can use the sentence patterns in this section and in 11.6.

Concession (with although, though, even though, whether … or)

1 Although the camera was expensive, Susan decided to buy it.

2 The game continued even though it was raining heavily.

3 Mrs Johnson won't sell her house whether you offer her $400,000 or not.

Condition   (with if, unless, on condition that, provided/ providing that)

4 If you don't water those plants, they will soon die.

5 The game won't be cancelled unless the field is flooded.

6 I'll lend you $100 provided that you repay the money by the end of the month.

Manner (with as if, as ... as, as though)

7 She ran as if tigers were chasing her.

8 John always works as hard as he can.

9 When Grandpa entered the room, he looked as though he had just seen a ghost.

Place (with where and wherever)

10 There's nobody hiding here. You can look wherever you like.

11 We decided to fish where two streams meet.

12 You can catch a bus where we waited last Thursday.

11.6 Adverbial expressions (2)

Check that you can use the sentence patterns shown below.

Purpose (with to, in order to/that, so that)

1 We had to shut the windows to keep the rain out.

2 Mary telephoned her friend in order to find out if her sister was better.

3 Peter went to an optician so that he could have his eyesight tested.

Reason (with because (of), since and as)

4 John was late for school this morning because the road was blocked by a traffic accident.

5 Since nobody else will inform the police, I will.

6 As a storm was approaching, we decided not to go fishing.

Note: 'As' and 'Since' can have more than one meaning, so try NOT to start a sentence with them. We can change (5) and (6) to become:

5a I will inform the police since nobody else will.

6a We decided not to go fishing as a storm was approaching.

Then the meaning of 'as' and 'since' is clear.

Result (with so, and so ... that)

7 We missed the last bus, so we had to walk home.

8 The camera was so expensive that Susan decided not to buy it.

9 The man spoke so quickly that we could not understand everything he said.

Time (with when, until, while, till, after, before, whenever)

10 Don't get off the bus until it stops.

11 We set out when the rain had stopped.

12 Mary had to wait until 4.30 p.m. before she could see the dentist.

Exercise 5

Choose the best words. XXX = no word is required.

1 We will arrive in time _____ our bus breaks down.

   A until   C even
   B unless   D providing

2 Although John had a headache, _____ he wanted to play football.

   A XXX   C yet
   B but   D however

3 Mary said, 'I won't buy the dress _____ you reduce the price.'

   A even   C as
   B since   D even if

4 The fishermen could not go out to sea _____ a tropical storm was approaching.

   A because of   C despite
   B unless   D as

5 You can go to your friend's house as _____ as you return before it is dark.

   A condition   B if   C providing   D long

6 Susan agreed to meet Mary where they _____ the previous week.

   A had met   B have met   C meet   D were met

7 Mary felt _____ tired that she lay down to have a rest.

   A very   B too   C so   D XXX

8 Don't turn the fan on until it _____ very hot.

   A has   B was   C will be   D is

12 Prepositions

1 Time expressions	*4* American and British usages
2 Preposition + pronoun	*5* Using prepositions (1)
3 No preposition needed	*6* Using prepositions (2)

12.1 Time Expressions

at + the exact time	John woke up at half past six.
in + a period of time	She came in the morning and left in the evening.
	Miss King was born in 1971.
on + a day	She was born on 21st November 1971.
	She had a party on her birthday. It was on Monday.
for + a length of time	We waited for twenty minutes.
since + a point of time	He hasn't been here since last Thursday.
no preposition before	last, next, this/that day, every, all, whole
	He phoned last night.
	She is arriving from London next Saturday.
	He usually phones every Monday (evening).

Exercise 1

Choose the right words to use. XXX = no preposition is needed.

1 We saw Susan _____ last Sunday.

   A on   B XXX   C in

2 We spoke to Mary _____ last Saturday afternoon.

   A XXX   B in   C on

3 We must leave _____ exactly five thirty.

   A XXX   B on   C at

4 Cancel the bill which we sent you _____ 25th June.

   A XXX   B on   C in

5 Aunty is coming _____ next Saturday morning.

A XXX   B in   C on

6 The new term begins _____ September.

A XXX   B in   C on

7 Our school year starts _____ September the fifth.

A on   B in   C XXX

8 _____ Saturday we went swimming.

A XXX   B In   C On

9 _____ Sunday afternoon, we went to the beach for a swim.

A XXX   B On   C In

10 She was born _____ the nineteenth century, _____ 1898, I think.

A in _____ in
B during _____ at
C at _____ in

11 We saw him at 3 p.m. _____ that day.

A XXX   B in   C at

12.2 Preposition + pronoun

This is a reminder. We saw in 4.1 that after a preposition we use the object form of a pronoun, i.e. me, him, her, us and them.

a   Between you and me, I think he is wrong.

b   This present is from Susan and me.

c   When you see John, tell him I have a letter for him.

Note: Many people wrongly use 'I' instead of 'me' in sentences like *a* and *b*.

12.3 No preposition is needed

Sometimes pupils put in a preposition when one is not needed. Sometimes they confuse the correct ways to use verbs and nouns. Compare these correct sentences:

1a They demanded an apology.

1b They made a demand for an apology.

2a We regretted the mistake.

2b We expressed our regret for the mistake.

3a You must emphasize that word.

3b You must put emphasis on that word.

4a They had a discussion about the problem.

4b They discussed the problem.

Exercise 2

Which words should be taken out of these wrong sentences?

1 He lacks in experience.

2 Mary is going to marry with her boyfriend next month.

3 If you want to ask a question, raise up your hand.

4 Some companies have lowered down the price of petrol.

5 I accompanied with my mother to the market yesterday.

6 Make sure you emphasize on the first syllable at that word.

7 You should omit out the 'e' in this word.

8 Please state out all your reasons clearly.

9 A stranger suddenly entered into the room.

10 Remove away all that rubbish immediately.

11 You should request for permission before you go out.

12 John resembles to his father very much.

13 The show ended up at half past ten.

14 Do you wish to add in any more comments?

15 The police will probably investigate into the cause of the fire.

16 Despite of the storm, we finished our game of football.

17 At the moment, the British pound equals to about US $1.50.

18 If the price exceeds beyond a reasonable figure, nobody will buy it.

19 You'd better contact with a company which can tell you the cost.

12.4 American and British usages

Some American expressions are different from British ones, e.g.

Some Americans say...	In British English we say ...
in behalf of	on behalf of
Sunday we went to see her.	On Sunday we went to see her.
We stayed Monday through Friday.	We stayed from Monday to Friday.

(Note: The American usage is better because it clearly includes Friday. We cannot tell from the British expression whether Friday is included or not.)

We went to visit with Mary.	We went to visit Mary.
Fill out this form.	Fill in this form.
Send it in care of Mary.	Send it care of Mary.
He protested the result.	He protested against the result.
different to that one.	different from that one

12.5 Using prepositions (1)

Check that you know the following uses of prepositions.

about *1* She told me about the quarrel.

2 $98.50 is about $100.

3 Do you know anything about stamp-collecting?

across We walked across the field to reach the river.

against *1* Stealing is against the law.

2 Don't lean against that wall. The pain is still wet.

along John noticed two men walking along the side of the road.

at *1* Susan is good at English.

2 Look at this flower.

3 What a nuisance. I've left my keys at home.

behind *1* When we were driving to the airport, Daddy noticed a police car behind us.

2 I sit behind Mary at school. She sits in front of me.

beside = at the side of   Father sat beside the taxi-driver.

besides = in addition to   There were four other boys at the
                            party besides Tom.

between *1* L comes between K and M in the alphabet.
         2 What's the difference between 'slim' and 'thin'?
         3 Share these bananas between the three of you.

by   *1* That picture was painted by a local artist.
         2 Uncle usually travels by bus or taxi.
         3 Did you make that table by yourself?
         4 John broke a window by accident.
         5 Who is that standing by your car?

for   *1* The woman thanked us for helping her.
         2 Shall we go for a walk?
         3 This letter is for Mother.
         4 Don't wait for me. I'll catch you up.

from   *1* Uncle has just arrived from Kingston.
         2 Two prisoners have escaped from prison.
         3 Did you borrow that bicycle from Ann?
         4 That letter is probably from Peter.

in   *1* Put all those things in the cupboard.
         2 You can leave that box in the corner of the room.
         3 Mother is in the living-room.
         4 Paul has a pain in his right leg.

of   *1* Two of these plates are cracked.
         2 Is this shirt made of cotton?
         3 That tin is full of flour.
         4 Hurry up! Get out of bed!

Exercise 3

Choose the best word each time. XXX = no word is needed.

1 Every day, a lot of people go to work _____ bus.

A on   B in   C by

2 In the alphabet, 'R' comes _____ 'Q' and 'S'.

A before   C between
B after

3 In square ABCD, side AB is _____ side CD.

A next to   C between
B behind   D opposite

4 Mary has a cold, so she is staying _____ home today.

A at   B in   C to

5 We can often see people walking _____ the road.

A among   B along   C cross

6 Leela has gone _____ shopping with Mother.

A to   B for   C XXX

7 The current here is very strong, so it is dangerous to try to swim _____ the river.

A into   C through
B across

8 John did not kick Tom _____ purpose. He kicked him _____ accident.

A by _____ by
B on _____ on
C on _____ by

9 Put that chair _____ the corner of the room.

A in   B on   C at

10 Yusof lives _____ the fifth floor _____ this block.

A in _____ in
B on _____ of
C in _____ of

11 If you are not _____ favour of the plan, you should vote _____ it.

A with _____ for
B in _____ against
C to _____ about

12 Here is the weather forecast _____ tomorrow.

A for   B about   C on

12.6 Using prepositions (2)

Check that you know the following uses of prepositions.

off	*1*	Three people got off the bus and two got on.
	2	Grandpa accidentally knocked a glass off the table.
on	*1*	Who is sitting on the sofa/settee next to Susan?
	2	Our office is on the tenth floor of the building.
	3	Sgt Johnson is on duty today.
	4	There's a black cat sitting on the wall.
over	*1*	The horse jumped over the hedge.
	2	The temperature is over 30° now.
	3	Peter tripped over the roots of a tree and fell down.
round	*1*	John chased his friend round a tree.
	2	Peter ran round the corner and bumped into a friend.
to	*1*	Mother often goes to the market.
	2	Please give this note to Vimala when you see her.
	3	Shall we invite Ann to the party?
	4	Hurry up! It's five to six already. We have to leave at six.
	5	Our team won by three goals to one.
towards		The plane ran into bad weather when it was flying towards New York.
under	*1*	Mr King paid under $12,000 for his car.
	2	If you are under 16, you can't take part in the competition.
	3	The cat is asleep under the table.
	4	Our boat went under three bridges.
	5	She won't sell her house under any conditions.
up		Several people have climbed up Mount Everest in recent years.
with	*1*	I often walk to school with my friend.
	2	We can cut through metal with a hacksaw.
	3	Mary has a black cat with white ears.
	4	Peter saw a neighbour arguing with a stranger.
	5	Johnny Gray lost his fight with Lennox Lewis.

without 1 Don't go without saying goodbye to Mary.

2 Nobody can live without water and food.

Exercise 4

Choose the best word each time.

1 Early _____ one morning, Mrs King heard a loud noise.

A in   B on   C XXX

2 Make adjectives _____ these nouns.

A from   B into   C to

3 Uncle came _____ Saturday evening and left _____ the next morning.

A in _____ in
B XXX _____ in
C on _____ XXX
D on _____ on

4 The heavy rain started at about six p.m. and stopped _____ an hour later.

A in   B on   C XXX

5 Father raised _____ his voice, so we knew that he was annoyed.

A XXX   B up   C in

6 At the Sports Meeting, Miss Menon recorded _____ the names of the winners.

A down   B XXX   C about

7 At night wild animals go out to seek _____ their food.

A XXX   B to   C for

8 When the tanker hit some rocks, two million _____ gallons of oil came out _____ the tanks.

A of _____ from
B XXX _____ of
C XXX off
D of _____ of

9 Mr King always sets _____ a good example _____ other people.

A XXX _____ for
B up _____ to
C off _____ to
D up _____ for

10 I saw it _____ my own eyes.

A by   B through   C with

11 We saw smoke _____ the distance.

A at   B in   C on

12 Miss Smith took no notice _____ the man.

A to   B at   C of

13 The firemen soon put the fire _____

A off   B out   C down

14 Take this medicine. It is good _____ you.

A for   B to   C with

13 Connectives

1 and, but, or, so	*4* either ... or
2 then, therefore, thus	*5* neither ... nor
3 although, though, since	*6* links between sentences

Connectives are words which link ideas. We can use conjunctions such as and, but, or and so to link ideas inside a sentence. In 13.6 we will consider connectives which link a pair of sentences.

13.1 and, but, or, so

and *1* Carrots and onions are vegetables.

 2 John is asleep and so is Grandpa.

but *3* Carrots are vegetables but bananas are fruit.

 4 John is asleep but Mary is reading a book.

or *5* Would you like an apple or an orange?

 6 Peter is cleaning his bicycle or repairing it.

so *7* The first bus was full, so we had to wait for another one.

 8 Those bananas are unripe, so you can't eat them.

13.2 then, therefore, thus

Compare these sentences and learn the right way to use 'then'.

wrong: Mary washed the dishes, then she put them away.

right: Mary washed the dishes and then she put them away.

right: Mary washed the dishes. Then she put them away.

We can use 'therefore' in these ways:

 Paul is 12 and John is 14. Therefore John is older than Paul.

 Paul is 12 and John is 14, and therefore John is older than Paul.

We can use 'thus' in the same ways as 'therefore' and in this way:

 Mary had a C in her test but Ann had an A, thus showing that Ann is better at English than Mary is.

Exercise 1

Choose the best word each time.

1 We're late, (but, or, so) we must hurry up.

2 My brother likes coffee (so, but, thus) my sister prefers tea.

3 Which do you prefer: chicken curry (and, but, or) fried rice?

4 Ann opened the envelope (but, and, then) read the letter carefully.

5 You can come with us if you like (and, or, but) stay at home.

6 Some girls are weaker than boys at mathematics (but, or, therefore) better than boys are at languages.

7 Peter planted the seeds in a row (then, and then, so) he watered them.

8 Mrs King turned off the light (and then, then, therefore) she went to bed.

9 I've lost my keys (but, and, or, so) somebody has stolen them.

10 Tigers are meat-eaters (or, so, but) deer eat grass and plants.

13.3 although, though, since

When we use these linking words, we do NOT need another connective.

right: Although Toyin is only 13, she is a very fast runner.

wrong: Although Toyin is only 13, but she is a very fast runner.

right: Since sea-water contains salt, we cannot drink it.

wrong: Since sea-water contains salt, so we cannot drink it.

We can use 'even' before 'though' (for emphasis) but we cannot use it before 'although' or 'since'.

> Even though his ankle was very painful, John continued to play football.

Exercise 2

Use the ideas in each pair of sentences to make one sentence containing 'Although' or 'although'.

1 Mary was very tired. She could not go to sleep quickly.

2 Peter tried his best. He did not win the race.

3 The shirt was slightly damp. John put it on.

4 Some snakes are poisonous. Many are quite harmless.

5 Uncle is very strict. He is quite kind-hearted.

13.4 either ... or

We can use 'either ... or' to emphasize that there is a choice. In most cases, we can omit 'either':

1a You can either stay here or come with us.

1b You can stay here or come with us.

2a Either John or Peter scored the winning goal.

2b John or Peter scored the winning goal.

13.5 neither ... nor

'Neither ... nor' gives a negative effect to verbs:

1 Neither the taxi-driver nor the lorry-driver was to blame for the accident.

2 Some large birds can neither fly nor swim.

3 This type of washing-machine is neither reliable nor cheap.

If a verb is already negative, use 'or' and not 'neither ... nor'.

4 Ann does not like coffee or tea.

5 That bus doesn't go to the railway station or the airport.

Exercise 3

Use the information in each pair of sentences to make one sentence containing 'either _____ or' OR 'neither _____ nor'.

1 You can go by bus. You can find a taxi.

2 Mary will help you. Susan will help you. (Ask one of them.)

3 We can go for a swim. We can go and visit Ann.

4 This driver wasn't going too fast. That driver wasn't going too fast.

5 Susan can't swim. She can't dive.

6 This type of bicycle isn't suitable for you. That type isn't suitable.

13.6 Links between sentences

We can start with this sentence:

> Kingston is a developing business centre.

We can add a second sentence in any of the following ways:

add information

in addition	also	another	this is not only
furthermore	too	besides	moreover

> Kingston is a developing business centre. Furthermore, it is becoming more and more important as a tourist and manufacturing centre.

repeat or emphasize the previous point

in fact	without doubt	There is no doubt that
indeed	definitely	It is clear that

> Kingston is a developing business centre. There is no doubt that it is one of the success stories of the Caribbean region.

give an example

for example	for instance
an example of this is ...	This can be seen ...

Kingston is a developing business centre. For example, it has become one of the leading financial centres of the region.

give a reason or explanation

The main reason for this ...	An important factor in this ...

> Kingston is a developing business centre. Two reasons for this are its stable government and hard-working people.

make a comparison or contrast

Compared with ...   However, ...

This is not the case ...   We cannot say this of ...

> Kingston is a developing business centre. However,
> there are other places in the region that have not been so
> successful.

changing the time

In the past,   Only forty years ago,   In the near future,

A century ago,   In the coming years,   Before long, it will ...

> Kingston is a developing business centre. Fifty years
> ago, it was largely undeveloped.

changing the place

In other parts of the world,   In Mexico, ...

In Trinidad, ...   In Britain, however, ...

showing a result

As a result,   One result of this development is
                                 that ...

Consequently,   Not surprisingly, ...

warning of a change (of attitude, ideas or topic)

However,   In spite of this, ...

Nevertheless,   Even so, we must remember
                                 that ...

There are many other ways of making a smooth change from one
sentence to another one.

Warning Don't use these connecting words too often. In many
cases, they are not necessary. Let them be your servants and not
your master.

Exercise 4

What connectives can you put in the blank spaces below to show a link between the ideas in each pair of sentences?

1 India and China are very densely populated. _____ there are still huge areas in Australia and Canada which contain few people.

2 Dogs help people in many ways. _____ , blind people often have a guide dog.

3 East winds from the sea may reach very high mountains and drop all their rain on the east side of them. _____ , the land on the other side of the mountains may receive little or no rain.

4 In modern times, most tourists travel in jumbo jets or in luxurious liners. _____travel was much more difficult, so fewer people visited foreign countries.

5 In the past ten years, some African countries have had several problems. _____ , in 1994, thousands (or perhaps millions) of people died in Rwanda.

6 Mary is a very kind-hearted and unselfish girl. _____, she often visits elderly neighbours to see if they need any help.

7 A war involving the use of atom bombs would threaten nearly everybody in the world. _____ , it would be a danger from which very few people could escape.

8 In Martinique, Mauritius and the former Indo-China, many people speak French. _____ in the Caribbean, Nigeria and India, English is more common than French.

9 Three of our best players could not play last night because they were ill. _____ , our team lost 3–1 against a team which it can normally beat.

10 The number of traffic accidents increases every year. _____ is that there are more and more vehicles on the roads.

14 Exclamations

Exclamations such as 'Oh!' and 'Ow!' are used to show strong feeling. (They are also called interjections.) Here are some examples. Notice that we use an exclamation mark after them.

Showing pain: Ow! Oh! Ouch!

Showing surprise: Oh! Ah!

Showing amusement: Ha! Ha!

Showing dislike
or disgust: Ugh!

Making an enquiry or
lack of understanding: Eh! Eh? Really?

Showing annoyance: Bah! Drat!

Exercise 1

When might people say these things?

1 Help! Help!

2 You naughty boy!

3 Stop! Don't move!

4 How kind of you!

5 What a silly thing to say!

6 Ow!

7 Hey!

8 Tut! Tut!

9 You liar!

10 Isn't she tall!

11 Look out!

12 Be quiet!

13 Be careful!

14 Don't be impatient!

15 Ouch!

16 Oooooh!

15 Abbreviations and Contractions

| *1* Abbreviations | *2* Acronyms | *3* Contractions |

15.1 Abbreviations

There are hundreds of abbreviations in use. You can find a long list of them at the back of a good dictionary. Check that you know the meaning of these abbreviations:

A.D.	Anno Domini = in the year of Our Lord (= after the birth of Christ)	Capt.	Captain
		cc	cubic centimetres
a.m.	ante meridiem = before noon	cf	compare
		CIA	Central Intelligence Agency
A.S.P.	Assistant Superintendent of Police	CID	Criminal Investigation Dept
B	black (of the lead in a pencil)	c.i.f.	cost, insurance, freight
		cm	centimetre
b.	born	Co.	company
B.A.	Bachelor of Arts	c/o	care of
BBC	British Broadcasting Corporation	C.O.D.	cash on delivery
		C. of E.	Church of England
B.C.	before Christ (was born)		
		Col.	Colonel
B.R.	British Rail(way)	Cpl.	Corporal
B.Sc.	Bachelor of Science	Cr.	credit(or)
		dept.	department
B.T.	British Telecom	do.	ditto (the same)
c.	circa = about	d/o	daughter of
C.	Celsius or Centigrade	doz.	dozen
caps.	capital letters	Dr.	doctor, debtor

96

EU	European Union	HMS	Her/His Majesty's Ship
e.g.	exempli gratia (= for example)	hon.	honorary, Honourable
ETA	estimated time of arrival	H.P.	hire purchase
		i/c	in charge
etc.	*et cetera* (= and others)	i.e.	*id est* = that is
		I.O.U.	I owe you
F.	Fahrenheit	IQ	intelligence quotient
FA	Football Association		
		ital	italics
fcap, fcp,	foolscap	J.P.	Justice of the Peace
f.o.b.	free on board		
Fr.	Father (in religion)	km	kilometre
ft	foot, feet	KO	knock-out
GB	Great Britain	L	learner (on a car)
GCE	General Certificate of Education	lb	pound(s) (weight)
		lbw	leg before wicket
GCSE	General Certificate of Secondary Education	lc	lower case (small letters)
		Lieut.	Lieutenant
GHQ	General Headquarters	Ltd.	Limited (of a company)
G.I.	government issue	m	metre, married, minute
gm	gramme(s)	M	Monsieur (French) (Mr)
GMT	Greenwich Mean Time		
GP	general practitioner (a doctor)	M.D.	Doctor of Medicine
		memo	memorandum
GPO	General Post Office	Messrs.	messieurs (gentlemen)
H	hard (of the lead in a pencil)		
		Mlle	Mademoiselle (Miss)
hi-fi	high fidelity		
		mm	millimetre

Mme	Madame (Mrs)	P.C.	Police Constable
MO	Medical officer *modus operandi* (of a criminal – method of doing something)	per cent	*per centum* (in each 100)
		p.l.c.	public limited co
		p.m.	*post meridiem* (after noon)
MP	Member of Parliament	P.O.	Post Office, Petty Officer
mpg	miles per gallon	pp	pages
mph	miles per hour	PRO	Public Relations Officer
Mr	Mister		
Mrs	Mistress	Prof	Professor
Ms	Miss or Mrs (= a female)	pro & con	*pro et contra* (= for and against)
MS	manuscript	pro tem	pro tempore (= temporarily; for the time being)
Mt	Mount(ain)		
n	neuter, noun		
NATO	North Atlantic Treaty Organization	PS	*post scriptum* (written after)
		PT	Physical Training
NB	nota bene (= note well)	Pte	private (soldier)
		PTO	please turn over
NCO	non-commissioned officer	PWD	Public Works Department
no.	number	Q.E.D.	*quod erat demonstrandum* (= which was to be proved)
np	(start a) new paragraph		
nr	near		
OHMS	On Her/His Majesty's Service	q.t.	on the q.t. = without other people knowing; secretly
OK	all correct		
oz	ounce	RAF	Royal Air Force
P	car park(ing)	R.C.	Roman Catholic
p.	page	rd	road
p.a.	*per annum* (annually)	re(f)	(with) reference (to)
		Rev.	Reverend
PAYE	Pay As You Earn		

R.I.P.	*requiescat in pace* (May he/she rest in peace [after death])	TUC	Trades Union Congress
RN	Royal Navy	TV	television
RSPCA	Royal Society for the Prevention of Cruelty to Animals	U.A.R.	United Arab Republic
NSPCC	National Society for the Prevention of Cruelty to Children	UK	United Kingdom
		UNESCO	United Nations Educational, Scientific and Cultural Organization
RSVP	*Répondez s'il vous plait.* (= Please reply.)	UNO	United Nations Organization
SAE	stamped, addressed envelope	USA	United States of America
Sgt	sergeant	v	versus (= against)
s/o	son of	VIP	very important person
SOS	(Help us.)	viz.	*videlicet* (= namely)
St.	Saint, street	YMCA	Young Men's Christian Association
Supt	Superintendent		
TB	tuberculosis		
TKO	technical knock-out	YWCA	Young Women's Christian Association
transpose	(= change the order of letters in a word)		

Exercise 1

What is the meaning of each of these abbreviations?

1 GP	*3* PTO	*5* Fr	*7* VIP	*9* caps.	*11* I.O.U.
2 PS	*4* a.m.	*6* P.C.	*8* NB	*10* c/o	*12* p.a.

At one time, people put a full stop after each letter of abbreviations such as these:

Mr.   Capt.   U.N.O.   Y.W.C.A.   P.T.O.

In modern times, most people omit the full stops, and write:

Mr   Capt   UNO   YWCA   PTO

You can put the full stops in or leave them out – as you wish.

15.2 Acronyms

An acronym is a word made by taking the first letters of other words, e.g.

ASAP   – as soon as possible
NATO   – North Atlantic Treaty Organisation
radar   – radio detection and ranging
laser   – light amplification by stimulated emission of radiation
ASEAN – Association of South-East Asian Nations
ONO   – or near offer
PAYE   – pay as you earn

15.3 Contractions

a Some common words are shortened forms of longer words, e.g.

bus	omnibus	phone	telephone
exam	examination	photo	photograph
gym	gymnasium	plane	aeroplane

b We use contractions when we speak and when we write down notes or what somebody said. Then we use short forms such as these:

I'm – I am	aren't – are not	they're – they are
he's – he is, he has	didn't – did not	can't – cannot
we've – we have	she'll – she will	won't – will not

Exercise 2

What is the full form of each of the following?

1 He'll come soon.

2 She'd better hurry.

3 Who'd done it?

4 I'm sure you're right.

5 They've just finished.

6 What's he done?

7 What's the matter?

8 She mightn't agree with you.

9 He said they'd already left.

10 You'd be caught if you attempted to escape.

16 Gerunds

1 Forms	2 Uses

16.1 Forms

Gerunds are a special kind of noun. They are made from verbs and can have an object. Many gerunds end in -ing.

Present Active	Present Passive
eating	Being eaten
I dislike biting garlic.	Being bitten by a lion is painful.
chewing	Being chewed

16.2 Uses

These examples show some of the common uses of gerunds.

a **As the subject of a verb.**

　　1 Swimming is a good form of exercise.

　　2 Smoking is very bad for you.

　　3 Taking part in outdoor games helps to keep you fit.

b **As the object of a verb**

　　1 Ann likes playing badminton with her friends.

　　2 Father hates being interrupted when he is reading a newspaper.

　　3 John prefers playing football to cricket.

c **After a preposition**

　　1 Most people will vote against raising taxes.

　　2 Miss Johnson is keen on playing the piano.

　　3 My sister is fond of growing flowers.

d Other uses

is used for	Lemon juice is used for writing messages in invisible ink.
	Spices are used for adding taste to food.
It's no good	It's no good complaining about the price.
It's useless	It's useless arguing with him.
It's a waste of time	It's a waste of time trying to get a taxi.
with a possessive adjective or a pronoun	Please excuse my arriving late.
or	Please excuse me arriving late. (more common)

e **After a verb**

Some verbs are often followed by a gerund, e.g.

1 Would you mind waiting a few minutes? (NOT 'to wait')

2 We look forward to meeting your friend. (NOT 'to meet')

3 Mother is used to cooking for a large family.

4 Susan dislikes going to bed late. (NOT 'to go')

Other verbs often followed by a gerund include these:

admitted losing	enjoy playing	prevent him from leaving
avoided meeting	finish cleaning	
burst out crying	give up smoking	propose increasing
considered leaving	can't help noticing	put off repairing
delayed paying	imagine winning	recommend renewing
deny refusing	keep on talking	can't stand eating
detest waiting	postpone playing	stop arguing
dislike eating	practise playing	

Warning Some verbs have one meaning when followed by a gerund, and a different meaning when followed by an infinitive. Compare these sentences:

1 I remember meeting her at Ann's party.

2 Remember to meet Susan at the railway station.

3 Have you already forgotten locking the door last night?

4 Did you forget to lock the door last night?

Exercise 1

Choose the best words each time.

1 Would you mind _____ this letter to Susan when you see her?

   A to give   B giving   C give

2 Do you know why Susan avoids _____ to us?

   A speaking   B to speak   C speak

3 Mary has gone to a commercial school _____ shorthand and typing.

   A to learn   B learn   C learning

4 Ann is sorry she made a mistake but she isn't used _____ dresses

   A to make   B to making   C making

5 Mr Johnson has no intention _____ us.

   A of helping   B to help   C help

6 Mrs King does not intend _____ them.

   A help   B helping   C to help

7 Nothing can stop time _____ by.

   A past   B passed   C passing

8 Mr Johnson has a large family to support, so he has nothing to do except _____ a living and get food and shelter for them.

   A earn   B earned   C earns

9 This advice will prevent you _____ a similar mistake later on.

   A to make   B make   C from making

10 That book is boring; it is not worth _____

   A reading   B to read   C read

11 All schools want their pupils _____ good results.

   A getting   B got   C to get

12 We look forward to _____ your new friend on Saturday.

   A meet   B have met   C meeting

17 Punctuation

1 full stop	*5* inverted commas	*9* dash
2 comma	*6* apostrophe	*10* capital letters
3 question mark	*7* colon	
4 exclamation mark	*8* semicolon	

17.1 Using a full stop

We put a full stop at the end of a sentence. Some people also put full stops after abbreviations. Many adult native-speakers are not sure when to use a full stop.

a When people speak, they do not always use complete sentences. When we write down their conversation, we put a full stop after each statement even when it is not a sentence.

Susan: Look at this postcard.

Paul: Who's it from?

Susan: Mary. She's in Europe.

Paul: Very nice. Nice stamps on it too.

b In continuous prose, English sentences MUST be

either (i) separated by a full stop, question mark, exclamation mark or semicolon

or (ii) joined by a connective such as and, but, so, when, etc.

Two sentences cannot be separated by a comma unless they are part of a list of three or more statements, etc.

Susan cut the bread, Ann put the butter on it, and then Mary put slices of cucumber on the bread.

A sentence cannot be chopped into two separate parts in this way:

wrong: We did not buy the fruit. Because it was too expensive.

right: We did not buy the fruit because it was too expensive.

Exercise 1

Correct any mistakes of punctuation in these sentences:

1 Peter is my best friend, he is very cheerful and generous.

2 Mary boiled the water, then she made tea for us.

3 Our car would not start, the battery was flat, that was very annoying.

4 The liquid turned litmus paper red, therefore it was an acid of some kind.

5 Mr Johnson noticed two men. Looking in the back of his car.

6 This is a valuable stamp, it must be worth over $1500.

7 Plymouth and Southampton are famous English ports, they are both on the south coast.

8 Uncle is coming on Saturday, he is driving from his home, I expect his wife and two daughters will come with him.

9 When the lights turned to green. We drove on towards the city.

10 Don't eat that plant, it can make you ill, it may even kill you if you eat enough of it.

17.2 Using commas

Study the following sentences carefully. Each of them shows a different use of the comma.

a Before and/or after the name of a person spoken to.

> Susan, what are you doing?
>
> Where are you going, Peter?
>
> It seems to me, Mary, that you are quite right.

b Between items in a list.

> He collects stamps, foreign coins, shells and other things.

c After a verb which introduces direct speech.

> She said, 'Hurry up or we'll miss the bus.'

d After direct speech if it is followed by a noun or pronoun and a speech verb.

> 'Hurry up or we'll miss the train,' he said.

e To make the meaning of a sentence clear to a reader.

'John chased Peter, and Frank ran after Paul.'

f To set off an expression which describes a preceding word. (This may be an expression in apposition or a non-defining clause.)

Mrs Johnson, the owner of the company, is a very successful designer.

g To mark off words such as 'indeed', 'however' and 'therefore' when they are inserted in a sentence.

Her plan looks good. Some people, however, claim that it is too expensive.

h To mark off a participle expression which does NOT refer to the word immediately before it. Compare the punctuation in these two sentences.

We watched a plane arriving from New York.

We watched a plane, wondering whether it would land safely or not.

Exercise 2

Put in commas, full stops and capital letters when necessary.

1 Mr Brown stared at the ceiling for a moment and then suddenly said 'All right you can borrow my car make sure you don't have an accident'

2 You can buy pineapples papayas melons and all sorts of vegetables at the market most of the fruit and vegetables are fresh and cheap.

3 'Father you're wanted on the phone' Mary said she told the caller that her father was coming then she got on with her work.

4 Susan rushed into the room nearly knocking Ann over as she did so Ann was surprised and not very pleased she wondered what had happened.

5 You should speak to Mr Johnson the manager of the shop he may be able to find a good job for you he has many friends in business.

17.3 Using a question mark

We use a question mark after a direct question but not after an indirect one.

direct: "What do you want?" she asked me.

indirect: She asked me what I wanted.

It is a common mistake to put a question mark after an indirect question.

Exercise 3

Put a full stop or a question mark after each of the following.

1 How do you do

2 How nice to meet you

3 How old is he

4 How kind of you

5 Had I known, I would have helped you

6 If she comes, where will she sleep

7 I wonder where Mary is now

8 I don't know where he works

9 John, are you ready yet

10 Try to find out how much it costs

11 Please can I have another one

12 That old car belongs to a neighbour but I doubt whether it is in working order

17.4 Using an exclamation mark

We saw in Chapter 14 that exclamation marks are used after exclamations, e.g.

Oh!   Ouch!   Ow!

They can also be used to show strong feeling:

Don't you dare do that again!   What a silly thing to say!

17.5 Inverted commas (speech marks, quotation marks)

We can use double inverted commas (" ...") or single ones (' ...').
Sometimes double inverted commas are more useful because they cannot be confused with an apostrophe.
Notice how the punctuation of direct speech is different when a speech verb interrupts a sentence as in (a) below.

a "Uncle will come this evening," Father said, "unless it rains heavily."

Sometimes speech occurs within speech:

c Susan said, "What did Mary say when you gave her the letter?"

Jane replied, "As far as I can remember, she said, 'That's good' or something like that."

When you write down dialogue, remember that each new speaker starts a new paragraph.

Exercise 4

Put in all necessary punctuation marks and capital letters.

1 did you enjoy yourselves on the beach mrs johnson asked mary yes thanks mary said but susan cut her foot how did she do that mrs johnson asked she trod on a sharp piece of glass mary said

2 mr and mrs jackson paused at the door on their way out will you be all right by yourself susan yes thanks susan replied dont worry about me shall I take a message if the phone rings yes mrs jackson said if anybody asks for father dont say hes out just say hes busy then take a message for him mr jackson nodded to his daughter yes thats right and dont tell anybody we are out

17.6 Using an apostrophe

a We can use an apostrophe to show that one or more letters is missing, as we saw in 15.3 e.g. didn't, can't, o'clock, won't, etc.

b When an apostrophe is used to show possession, you can follow these guidelines:

(i) Add 's to a singular noun: Mary's key, the woman's car

Add 's to a plural noun which does not end in 's': the women's voices, a children's playground, the fishermen's boats.

(ii) Add ' to a plural noun: the girls' bicycles, the players' names

singular or plural but not ending in 's'	plural
the woman's voice	the ladies' voices
the women's dresses	my friends' clothes
in an hour's time	in two hours' time
a day's delay	three days' delay
the player's name	the players' names

Warning: We use an apostrophe only to show that letters have been left out OR to show possession. We do not add an apostrophe to verbs or to plural words when there is no possession. In many cases, we use an apostrophe for people and common animals. In other cases, we use 'of':

right	wrong
the back of the bus	the bus's back
the side of the car	the car's side

Exercise 5

Put in apostrophes when necessary. In some sentences, no apostrophes are needed.

1 Two of our teachers have red cars.

2 My cousin lives near us but travels to the town every day because he works as a police officer there.

3 At the end of this month, we will have two weeks holiday.

4 That is not Marys watch. It must be somebody elses watch.

5 Several of my friends are going to a childrens concert in a weeks time.

6 Listen! I can hear mens voices outside. They are arguing about the results of some football matches. Ah, now I can hear a womans voice too.

7 Mother won't be long. She has gone to buy some vegetables. She should be back in a few minutes time.

8 Uncles car is a white one but Mrs Jacksons car is green.

9 Newtown High School is a girls school, not a boys school.

10 Video games are more popular with boys than with girls.

Exercise 6

Change these expressions to show possession. Put in an apostrophe only OR 's OR use of.

1 my sister – friend

2 my sisters – friends

3 my father – car

4 the box – the side

5 my brother – address

6 her uncle – house

7 John – left leg

8 the tree – the root

9 the car – the front

10 my cousin – friend

11 two months – holiday

12 a few days – rest

13 the train – the driver

14 the passengers – bags

15 the baby toys

16 the children – party

17 the dress – the belt

18 the shirt – the collar

19 the sun – rays

20 the room – the temperature

17.7 Using a colon (:)

a A colon can give details of a word before it.

1 Vimala has three hobbies: running, playing games and singing.

2 Mary had many things to do: sweep the floor, wash the clothes, wash the dishes and put them away, dust the furniture, etc.

3 This island has many advantages: fine beaches, beautiful scenery, good shops and excellent hotels.

4 Use three of the following in sentences of your own:

mischief   fortunate   eventually   scorched   diluted

b Some people use a colon before direct speech or quotation, and after the greeting in a letter.

1 She waited a moment and then said: "The house is worth more than that."

2 (At the start of a letter) Dear Miss King:

17.8 Using a semicolon(;)

The main use of a semicolon is to replace a full stop between sentences when we feel that the two sentences are closely connected. Many writers rarely use a semicolon.

1 It began to grow dark, and a chilly breeze swept in from the sea; we knew it was time to go home.

2 Peter got out of bed and looked out of the window; he wondered what kind of a day lay ahead of him.

17.9 Using a dash

A single dash marks a break in a sentence. The writer wants the reader to pause for a moment before reading the rest of the sentence.

a Saturday was a day Pauline would always remember – a day which brought her everlasting joy.

b She moved steadily from shop to shop, not merely looking but buying and buying – something she had never been able to do before.

Some writers use a pair of dashes in the same way as a pair of brackets, i.e. to mark off information which is not essential in a sentence.

c She paused outside Brimleys — the biggest and most expensive store in town — and then plunged in, determined to buy anything which caught her fancy.

d She tried on — and rejected — more than a dozen pairs of shoes before she found something that was both smart and comfortable.

17.10 Using capital letters

The word 'I' is always written with a capital letter. Newspapers often use capital letters for all the words in a headline on the front page. In addition, we use capital letters at the beginning of the following:

a the first word in a sentence

b the first word of direct speech (dialogue)

c when introducing a quotation

d a title or rank (Major Johnson)

e proper nouns, e.g. names of people, days, months, roads, cities, etc.

f proper adjectives, e.g. the Brazilian jungle, the Kenyan capital, etc.

g (sometimes) for each new line of poetry

h exclamations such as 'Ow!' and 'Ah!'

i when using a pronoun to refer to God, Christ, Allah or a sacred person in a religion, and to sacred books such as the Bible, the Koran, etc.

j Organizations such as UNO, the YMCA, the RSPCA, etc.

k words such as Uncle, Aunt, Inspector and Sergeant when they refer to a person and do not have words such as my, his or her before them. Compare these correct sentences:

(i) We saw Uncle sitting in the car.

(ii) I saw my uncle sitting in the car.

(iii) I think Mother is just coming.

(iv) Susan saw her mother approaching the house.

Exercise 7

Imagine that the following words are used in the middle of a sentence.
Underline the words which should start with a capital letter.

1 angry, gold, silver, buses, clock, sunday, canada, susan, photograph, video

2 education, school, teacher, pupil, english, india, african, atlantic ocean

3 october, tuesday, christmas, easter, southern, spanner, drill, kitchen, home

4 television, satellite, mars, his uncle, caribbean, jamaica, market street

5 eagle, london, trinidad, the olympic games, dentist, explosion, tokyo, washington

6 peter's friends, european, the daily mail (a newspaper), the bay of biscay

7 in singapore, on monday evening, diamonds, the rex hotel, our doctor, dr king

8 february, afro-american, the royal air force, a ford car, the philippine eagle

18 Spelling

1	Points in previous chapters	*6*	adding final -ing
2	'ei' and 'ie'	*7*	American spelling
3	-ar, -er, -or	*8*	final -y
4	doubling a consonant	*9*	silent letters
5	adding a prefix	*10*	difficult pairs

18.1 Points in previous chapters

Please see previous chapters of words ending in these ways:

a	-os, -oes	3.1(4)		*d*	-ce, -se	3.7
b	-eys, -ies	3.6(6-7)		*e*	-nce, -nt	5.3
c	-ful(ly)	11.4		*f*	-fs, -ves	3.1(5)

18.2 Words containing 'ei' and 'ie'

Rule: Write 'ei' after 'c'. Write 'ie, after other letters. Notice that this rule can be used only when 'ei' and 'ie' are spoken with the /ee/ sound. A common exception to the rule is 'seize'. Check that you can spell these words:

ei   receive, receipt, deceive, conceited, ceiling, foreign, leisure, their, neighbour, weight, height, freight

ie   believe, achieve, niece, piece, friend, view, field, society, science, ancient, shriek, belief, thief

Your teacher or somebody else can test you on the above words. Spell some of them without looking at the book.

18.3 Words ending in -ar, -er or -or

The letters -ar, -er and -or at the end of the following words are pronounced in the same way with the sound of -er in 'driver'. Check that you can spell these words:

-ar beggar, scholar, regular, popular, cellar, vicar, pillar, pedlar, liar

-er swimmer, winner, driver, reporter, speaker, dancer, fighter, painter

-or governor, collector, instructor, professor, sculptor, actor, bachelor

113

Exercise 1

Put in the missing letters:

1 sug.r	*5* inspect.r	*9* tail.r	*13* rec..ved	*17* h..ght
2 doct.r	*6* explor.r	*10* regist.r	*14* for..gner	*18* soc..ty
3 farm.r	*7* burgl.r	*11* mort.r	*15* n..ghbour	*19* th..ves
4 coll.r	*8* visit.r	*12* carpent.r	*16* c..ling	*20* l..sure

18.4 Doubling a consonant

Try to understand the difference between a short vowel and a long vowel.

You can hear short vowels That pen is not much good.
in these words:

You can hear long vowels Pa, may we all go too?
in these words:

When we add -ed or -ing to a word, we double the consonant if a short vowel comes before it. We do NOT double the consonant if a long vowel comes before it.

short vowels: stopped, grinned, stepped, hopped, cutting, winning

long vowels: hoped, shining, feeding, farming, waded, voting

18.5 Adding a prefix

These examples show you when we have a double consonant near the front of a word.

dis + agree = disagree   un + necessary + unnecessary

dis + solve + dissolve   un + happy = unhappy

dis + appear = disappear   un + usual = unusual

When we add 'all' to the front of a word, we leave out an 'l' as in these words:

all + though = although all + ways = always all + together = altogether

all + ready = already   all + mighty = almighty   all + most = almost

18.6 Adding final -ing

Omit a final silent 'e' when you add -ing:

write – writing	make – making	hope – hoping
shine – shining	dine – dining	phone – phoning

Notice that we keep a final 'e' if a word ends in -ee, -oe or -ye

see – seeing	canoe – canoeing	dye – dyeing

If a word ends in a vowel or consonant + 'y', keep the 'y' when you add -ing.

carry – carrying	study – studying	worry – worrying
marry – marrying	deny – denying	rely – relying
play – playing	buy – buying	

18.7 American spelling

The following table shows some of the differences between American and British spelling.

British	American
metre, centre, theatre	meter, center, theater
colour, honour, behaviour	color, honor, behavior
programme, skilful	program, skillful
cheque, aluminium	check, aluminum
travelled, quarrelled	traveled, quarreled

Exercise 2

Add- ing to these words:

1 fit	*4* fry	*7* wrap	*10* study	*13* rob	*16* let
2 live	*5* win	*8* eat	*11* move	*14* sit	*17* shut
3 clean	*6* get	*9* begin	*12* judge	*15* rain	*18* wake

Exercise 3

Make words of opposite meaning by adding one of the prefixes in the box.

dis	il	im	in	ir	non	un

1 possible	*4* flammable	*7* regular	*10* similar	*13* literate
2 known	*5* convenient	*8* obey	*11* natural	*14* fasten
3 legal	*6* member	*9* mobile	*12* capable	*15* probable

18.8 Final -y

When forming the plural of a word ending in 'y', (3.1)

vowel + 'y'   –   'ys'   as in valleys, days, monkeys and donkeys

consonant + 'y   –   'ies'   as in babies, cities, ladies and bodies

When adding -ing, keep the 'y', (18.6)

carry – carrying   buy – buying

play – playing   study – studying

Except as above, change final 'y' to 'i' when adding a suffix.

busy – business   tidy – tidily   heavy – heavily
happy – happiness   busy – busily   pretty – prettily

(There are some exceptions but they are not important here.)

18.9 Words containing silent letters

Check that you can spell the following words and know what they mean. Each of them contains at least one letter which is nearly silent or completely silent when we say the word.

b– doubtful, climb, climbing, numb, dumb, debt, bomb

c– muscle, conscious, discipline

d– Wednesday, handsome, grandmother

g– gnat, gnaw, reign, sign, design, foreigner

h– exhibition, vehicle, honest, rhyme, exhaust(ed)

k– knee (l), knife, knit, knowledge, knuckles

l– calm, talk, walk, half, salmon

n– autumn, column, condemn

p– cupboard, receipt, pneumonia, psalm

r– forget, sarcastic, heart, sailor, iron

s– island

t– often, soften, listen, moisten, Christmas

w– sword, answer, wrist, wrong, wrinkle, wreck

Exercise 4

Complete these sentences by putting in one of the above words containing a silent letter.

1 There is water all round land which is an _____

2 A monkey can _____ up a tree much faster than a boy can.

3 Women sometimes use wool and needles to _____ a pullover or jumper.

4 People can keep books, clothes or food in a _____ . There was nothing in hers when Mother Hubbard looked in it.

5 Is _____ the third or fourth day of the week?

6 There are poisonous gases in the _____ fumes of a car or lorry.

7 _____ is a serious illness which can kill people, especially elderly ones.

8 If you clench your fist, you can see your _____

9 If you are in _____, you owe money to somebody.

10 'Play' and 'grey' _____ but 'play' and 'grow' do not.

18.10 Difficult pairs

Exercise 5

Make sure that you know the difference between each pair of words below.

Then answer the questions about the words.

1 principal, principle

To help you remember the spelling, learn "The P _____ is my pal." What is the missing word?

2 cereal, serial

Which one can we eat? Which one may be in a book or on television?

3 whether, weather

Which one can refer to rain and sunshine?

4 affect, effect

Put in the missing words: '_____' is usually a verb but

'_____' is usually a noun. Did the storm have much _____ on the town? (Put in the missing word.)

5 desert, dessert

Which one can we eat?

6 die, dye (dying, dyeing)

Mary wants to _____ her blouse green. What is the missing word?

7 flour, flower

By grinding up seeds, we can make _____ from rice, wheat and maize.

8 pail, pale

Which one can also be called 'bucket'?

9 pass, passed, past

One of these words is NEVER a verb. Which is it?

10 waist, waste

We can put a belt round one of these. Which one is it?

11 new, knew

Which one is the past form of a verb?

12 hear, here

Which one might make you think of your ears?

13 their, they're, there

Which one can mean 'belonging to them'?

14 beach, beech

Where can you often see a lot of sand?

15 bare, bear

Which one can kill you? What does the other word mean?

16 currant, current

Which one can be found in the sea or in a river? Which one grows on a bush and can be used in a cake?

19 American English

Most words in American English and British English are the same but some differences are shown below.

British	American
ten past four 4.10	ten after four
five to six 5.55	five before six
bank holiday	public holiday
bill (restaurant)	check
biscuit	cookie or cracker
block of flats	apartment house
bonnet (car)	hood
book (accommodation)	reserve
boot (car)	trunk
car park	parking lot
corridor	hall
cupboard	closet
curtains	drapes
decorator	house painter
drawing pin	thumb tack
dressing-gown	bathrobe
dummy (baby's)	pacifier
dustman	garbage collector
gear lever	shift
goods train	freight train
engine-driver	engineer
(school) hall	auditorium
handbag	purse
jelly	jello
kennel	doghouse
lavatory	toilet
lift (n)	elevator
lorry	truck/van

nappy	diaper
pant(ie)s	briefs
paraffin	kerosene
petrol	gas(oline)
postman	mailman
purse	coin purse
railway	railroad
rubbish	garbage
saloon (car)	sedan
shop	store
single (ticket)	one-way (ticket)
return (ticket)	round trip (ticket)
sleeper (on a railway track)	tie
tap	faucet
trousers	pants
toilet	restroom
vest	undershirt
waistcoat	vest
wallet	billfold
zed	zee
nought	zero

1 What does an American want if he asks to buy (a) drapes, (b) some gas, (c) some pants, (d) a sedan, (e) some diapers?

2 What is an American woman looking for if she asks the way to (a) the elevators, (b) a restroom, (c) the nearest faucet, (d) the auditorium?

20 Animals and Fish

You will find many lists of animals, flowers, fruit and other things in this book. Ask and answer questions about things in the lists. For example, you can ask:

Q: In list 1, which animal flies around in the dark and eats insects?

You can give a clue if you like, e.g.

Q: In list 1, which animal likes to eat honey? Its name starts with 'b'.

List 1	List 2	List 3	List 4
anteater	elephant	leopard	racoon
antelope	ferret	lion	rat
ape	fox	llama	reindeer
badger	gazelle	mole	rhinoceros
bat	gerbil	mongoose	seal
bear	giraffe	monkey	sheep
beaver	goat	moose	shrew
buffalo	gopher	mouse	skunk
bull	gorilla	mule	sloth
camel	guinea pig	orangutan	squirrel
cat	hamster	otter	stoat
chipmunk	hare	ox	tapir
cougar	hedgehog	panda	tiger
cow	hippopotamus	panther	wallaby
coyote	horse	pig	walrus
deer	hyena	platypus	weasel
dingo	jackal	porcupine	whale
dinosaur	jackass	possum	wildebeest
dog	jaguar	puma	yak
donkey	kangaroo	rabbit	zebra

Here are the names of some fish. Can you think of any more names?

bass	goldfish	perch	skate
catfish	gudgeon	pike	sole
cod	guppy	plaice	stickleback
dace	haddock	ray	sturgeon
dogfish	halibut	roach	swordfish
eel	herring	salmon	trout
flounder	mackerel	sardine	tuna
flying-fish	minnow	shark	whiting

21 Antonyms (opposites)

Warning When you study antonyms (words of opposite meaning) in this chapter, remember that a word can have several meanings and therefore several antonyms. For example, notice possible antonyms for 'beautiful':

a beautiful face	antonym: ugly
a beautiful day	antonym: horrible, unpleasant
a beautiful goal	antonym: clumsy, crude
a beautiful poem	antonym: unattractive, unpleasant, plain

We learn from this that many of the antonyms given below may not always be suitable or correct.

In the following lists, match each word in the box with an antonym taken from the lists.

List 1

alkali	boo	dead	below	retreat	gradually	slow down
prevent	deny	never	awake	decline	reasonable	deliberate
natural	defend	pleased	modern	presence	shortage	departure

acid	attack	admit	asleep	above	accelerate	arrival
alive	advance	allow	angry	accept	abruptly	accidental
absurd	always	applaud	ancient	absence	artificial	abundance

List 2

dull	well	stern	worse	curse	neither	in front of
sell	end	sharp	small	timid	forwards	cowardly
top	good	front	sweet	narrow	civilised	straight

buy	bow	broad	bless	begin	bent	bitter
bad	back	bold	blunt	bright	better	barbaric
big	brave	both	badly	behind	bottom	backwards

List 3

hot	free	dirty	hero(ine)	expand	expensive	miserable
go	warm	reveal	destroy	foolish	reckless	separate
can	wrong	modest	simple	release	excitedly	voluntary

cold	cheap	clever	calmly	coward	combine	conceited
cool	come	conceal	capture	correct	contract	compulsory
clean	create	captive	cannot	complex	cautious	cheerful

List 4

up	exit	go up	sober	certain	sunset	shallow
wet	easy	cheap	night	safety	victory	encourage
late	full	flood	friend	similar	lighten	multiply

dry	deep	down	empty	defeat	divide	discourage
day	early	drunk	enemy	darken	difficult	doubtful
dear	dawn	danger	drought	descend	different	entrance

List 5

thin	last	past	near	strong	villain	light
lose	soft	wise	many	solid	hinder	innocent
lost	love	true	stale	proud	heaven	unknown

far	hero	find	found	feeble	guilty	foolish
few	help	hard	fresh	famous	hatred	hollow
fat	hell	false	future	first	heavy	humble

List 6

war	poor	wealthy	smooth	wealth	noisily	singular
slow	eager	scarce	forget	private	unripe	temporary
rude	urban	rarely	slowly	reward	include	pessimism

omit	ripe	rapid	peace	poverty	quietly	optimism
poor	rough	polite	plural	plentiful	reluctant	permanent
rich	rural	often	punish	quickly	remember	public

List 7

wide	tiny	guilt	untidy	set free	minimum	hard-working
high	short	lazy	quietly	majority	stationary	extinguish
sane	adult	senior	superior	feminine	spendthrift	knowledge

low	long	loudly	moving	maximum	imprison	industrious
mad	miser	idle	narrow	minority	juvenile	innocence
neat	junior	ignite	inferior	immense	ignorance	masculine

Exercise 1

Form words opposite in meaning to the following words by adding prefixes such as

dis, il, im, in, ir, non and un.

1 perfect	5 obedient	9 believe	13 advantage	17 employed
2 official	6 aware	10 sense	14 obey	18 legal
3 approve	7 available	11 conscious	15 placed	19 possible
4 active	8 able	12 correct	16 welcome	20 regular

Exercise 2

Form opposites by changing the ending of the following words. Change -ful to -less.

1 useful	4 powerful	7 hopeful	10 shameful
2 careful	5 doubtful	8 painful	11 thoughtful
3 helpful	6 cheerful	9 harmful	12 restful

Exercise 3

Form opposites by adding a prefix from the box to one of the words below. Use each prefix to form the antonym of TWO separate words.

dis	im	in	ir	un

1 kind   *3* proper   *5* relevant   *7* adequate   *9* responsible

2 wise   *4* audible   *6* qualify   *8* practical   *10* believe

Exercise 4

Give antonyms for the words in **bold** type below.

1 Last month was **warmer** than expected.

2 Yesterday was the **hottest** day of the year so far.

3 Taxes are likely to **decrease** next year.

4 Some judges are quite **lenient** and dislike sending people to prison.

5 The firemen think that the fire was started **accidentally**.

6 The man **denied** that he had been driving too fast.

7 This problem is quite **complicated**.

8 That medicine may be **beneficial** or it may not be.

9 If meat is **tough**, be careful how you cook it.

10 What a **beautiful** day!

22 Bicycles

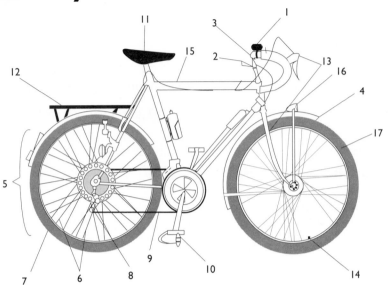

Parts of a bicycle

Study the diagram and the list of parts below. Then write by each part the number which identifies it in the diagram.

____ bell   ____ spokes   ____ saddle

____ handle-bar   ____ wheel   ____ carrier

____ brake(s)   ____ rim of a wheel   ____ light

____ chain   ____ tyre   ____ mudguard

____ gears   ____ valve   ____ pedal

____ gear-lever   ____ frame

Questions

1 How can you raise or lower the saddle?

2 What are the gears for?

3 What are the valves for?

4 What do racing cyclists fix to their pedals? Why?

5 John is cycling down a steep hill. What will happen if he puts on his front brake but not his rear brake?

6 About 100 years ago, a bicycle was called a 'Penny Farthing'. Try to find out why it had this name.

23 Birds, Insects and Trees

23.1 Birds

Can you describe any of the birds in these lists? What do they eat?
Where do they live? Do you know the names of any more birds?

List 1	List 2	List 3	List 4	Parts of a bird
blackbird	flycatcher	owl	sparrow hawk	wings
budgerigar	goose	parrot	starling	beak
buzzard	grouse	partridge	stork	tail
canary	hawk	pelican	swallow	feathers
chaffinch	heron	penguin	swan	breast
crow	jackdaw	pheasant	swift	talons
cuckoo	jay	pigeon	thrush	eyes
dove	kingfisher	puffin	tit	legs
duck	magpie	raven	turkey	claws
eagle	moorhen	robin	vulture	
falcon	mynah	rook	wagtail	
finch	nightingale	seagull	woodpecker	
flamingo	nuthatch	sparrow	wren	

Questions

1 Which bird catches mice at night?

2 Name four birds which kill and eat smaller birds.

3 Which bird is sometimes used for races (and to carry messages)?

4 Which birds eat fish but don't swim in, on or under the water?

Ask and answer more questions.

127

23.2 Insects

List 1	List 2	List 3	List 4
ant	cicada	flea	midge
aphid	cockroach	fly	mosquito
bee	cricket	gnat	moth
beetle	daddy-long-legs	grasshopper	termite
bug	dragonfly	horsefly	wasp
butterfly	earwig	locust	weevil
centipede	fire-fly	louse	

Questions

1 In each of the four lists, which of the insects have you seen? Where did you see them?

2 Which insect(s) can we sometimes see in these places?

    a In a sack of rice.

    b On a dog's back.

    c Flying towards or round a light at night.

    d Running on the kitchen floor at night.

23.3 Trees

List 1	List 2	List 3	List 4	List 5
apple	chestnut	hazel	oak	poplar
ash	citrus	holly	olive	redwood
banyan	cypress	laburnum	palm	rowan
beech	elder	larch	pear	spruce
birch	elm	lime	pine	sycamore
cedar	hawthorn	maple	plane	walnut
cherry		mulberry	plum	willow

Questions

1 Can you think of the names of any more trees?

2 From which tree do acorns come?

3 From which tree are cricket bats made?

4 Which trees produce fruit which people eat?

5 Which tree is used by farmers who produce silk from silk-worms?

Exercise 1

Put in the name of a bird, an insect, a tree or parts of a bird.

1 A _____ can produce its own light at night.

2 A _____ tree produces many red berries before Christmas and has prickly leaves.

3 A small bird has _____ at the end of its legs but a large bird such as an eagle has _____ so that it can tear meat to pieces.

4 A female _____ can spread malaria by biting people.

5 A swarm of _____ can eat all the vegetation in their path.

6 The smallest bird in the four lists is a _____ but a humming-bird is even smaller.

7 We get walnuts from a _____ tree, and olives from an _____ tree.

8 The 'cows' which ants 'milk' and look after on plants are _____

9 A _____ may be 4–6 cm long and is often seen by rivers or ponds. It has large wings.

10 Oranges and lemons grow on _____ trees.

24 Parts of the Body

Parts of the body

Identify the parts of the body by writing the correct number by each part on this page.

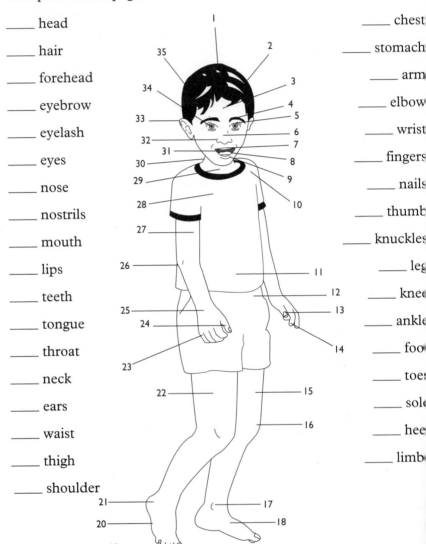

_____ head	_____ chest
_____ hair	_____ stomach
_____ forehead	_____ arm
_____ eyebrow	_____ elbow
_____ eyelash	_____ wrist
_____ eyes	_____ fingers
_____ nose	_____ nails
_____ nostrils	_____ thumb
_____ mouth	_____ knuckles
_____ lips	_____ leg
_____ teeth	_____ knee
_____ tongue	_____ ankle
_____ throat	_____ foot
_____ neck	_____ toes
_____ ears	_____ sole
_____ waist	_____ heel
_____ thigh	_____ limb
_____ shoulder	

Where can you find these things INSIDE a body?

a heart *b* kidneys *c* lungs *d* an artery *e* veins

25 Parts of a Car

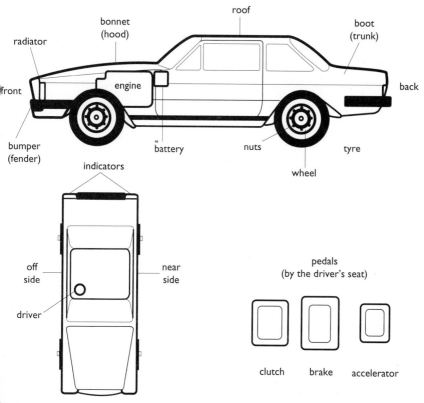

Where can you find the following in a car? What are they used for?

1 the windscreen (US windshield)

2 the windscreen wiper(s)

3 the gear lever (US shift)

4 the odometer (for distance)

5 the speedometer (for speed)

6 a sun roof

7 the fuel gauge

8 seat belts

9 the ignition

10 the steering wheel

11 the horn

12 the heating system

Note: In the UK and some other countries, motorists drive on the left. In the USA, France, Germany and many other countries, motorists drive on the right.

Find out what a motorist might use these things for:

a a tyre gauge   b a jack   c a jump lead   d a tow(ing) rope/cable

131

26 Clothing and Foot-wear

Check that you know what these things are:

List 1	List 2	List 3	List 4
a shirt	a cardigan	a jacket	a skirt
a vest	a sweater	a tunic	trousers
a blouse	a pullover	a waistcoat	slacks
a top	a scarf	a blazer	jeans
a dress	gloves	a suit	pyjamas
pant(ie)s	a belt	a coat	a night-dress
briefs	socks	a raincoat	a night-gown
a slip (a petti-coat)	stockings	an overcoat	a dressing-gown
	tights	a macintosh (a mac)	a bath-robe
	a T-shirt		

List 5

shoes, boots, slippers, sandals, slip-slops, loafers, Wellington boots, suede shoes

Exercise 1

What are these things? Who might wear them?

1 a spacesuit
2 a sari
3 a helmet
4 a uniform
5 a gown
6 swimming trunks
7 a bathing costume
8 a turban
9 a sarong
10 a cheung sam
11 a fez
12 a yashmak
13 thigh boots
14 a track suit
15 a bikini

Exercise 2

What might these people wear?

1 the pilot of a plane
2 a bride at a wedding
3 a nurse at a hospital
4 a fireman
5 an underwater photographer
6 a football player

27 Colours

1 Colours	*2* Light and dark	*3* Idioms with colours

27.1 Colours

A Check that you know what colours the following are:

black	white	crimson	blue	gold
brown	pink	purple	green	silver
grey	red	mauve	orange	
cream	scarlet	violet	yellow	

B Find out what these colours look like:

aquamarine	buff	charcoal	sapphire	indigo	lilac
mahogany	ruby	emerald	maroon	lemon	sepia

The manufacturers of paints, lipsticks, cars and clothes have their own names for shades of colours. For example, shades of green include these:

Apple green	Deep green	Grass green	Middle green
Brilliant green	Light green	Island green	Vivid green
Brunswick green	Olive green	Neptune green	Emerald green

Exercise 1

What colour are the following?

1 unripe bananas	6 rice	11 oranges
2 over-ripe bananas	7 smoke	12 lemons
3 your eyes	8 grass	13 chocolate
4 your hair	9 the sky	14 the sea
5 coconut	10 the moon	15 pearls

27.2 Light and dark

When we need to be more accurate, we can use 'light', 'pale', 'dark' and 'deep' before many colours:

a Tomatoes are green at first. Then they turn pale yellow before they become light red, then red and finally dark red.

b John has pale blue eyes; they are almost grey.

We can also add -ish to some colours:

c Sometimes the sea has a greyish green look.

27.3 Idioms with colours

There are many expressions in which we use colours, e.g.

the black market – an unofficial and sometimes illegal
market in which scarce goods are
sold at a high price

a red herring – something intended to deceive people
(or animals)

Exercise 2

Match the expressions with their meanings,

List 1

expressions	meanings (in the wrong order)
1 red tape	*a* a list of people or firms who will be penalised
2 a black list	*b* an inexperienced person; a novice
3 a greenhorn	*c* in a position of good fortune and/or wealth
4 in the purple	*d* delays caused by official procedures
5 yellow at heart	*e* a sign of cowardice
6 a white feather	*f* cowardly, frightened of something

List 2

1 whitewash
2 a white lie
3 with green fingers
4 once in a blue moon
5 looking as black as thunder
6 caught red-handed

a caught breaking the law
b looking extremely angry
c something intended to deceive and conceal
d good at gardening and growing things
e very rarely or hardly ever
f an untruthful statement made with good intentions

List 3

1 yellow press
2 green with envy
3 blue-collar workers
4 a red rag to a bull
5 as white as a sheet
6 blackmail

a very jealous or envious of something
b very frightened or ill
c papers of a low standard
d something which greatly annoys somebody
e people who do not work in an office, i.e. manual workers
f illegally making somebody pay money or do something in return for not making public bad information about them

28 Countries, Capitals, etc

1 Continents
2 Countries, Capitals, Languages and People

28.1 Continents

People do not always agree on the number and names of continents. Some people say that there are five continents: Africa, North and South America, Asia, Australia and Europe.
Other people say that there are seven continents: Africa, North America, South America, Antarctica, Asia, Australia (or Australasia) and Europe.

Exercise 1

In which continent is each of the following?

1 Greece *3* Thailand *5* Eire   *7* Namibia *9* Bangladesh

2 Peru   *4* Cambodia *6* Canada *8* Portugal *10* Kenya

28.2 Countries, Capitals, Languages and People

Check that you know the following. They are some (but not all) of the countries in the world.

Country	Capital	Language	A person
Algeria	Algiers	Arabic	an Algerian
Argentina	Buenos Aires	Spanish	an Argentinean
Australia	Canberra	English	an Australian
Austria	Vienna	German	an Austrian
Barbados	Bridgetown	English	a Barbadian
Belgium	Brussels	Flemish, French	a Belgian
Bolivia	La Paz	Spanish	a Bolivian
Brazil	Brasilia	Portuguese	a Brazilian
Burma	Rangoon	Burmese	a Burmese
Canada	Ottawa	English, French	a Canadian
Chile	Santiago	Spanish	a Chilean
China	Beijing	(Mandarin) Chinese	a Chinese man or woman
Cuba	Havana	Spanish	a Cuban
Denmark	Copenhagen	Danish	a Dane
Egypt	Cairo	Arabic	an Egyptian
England	London	English	An Englishman (or woman)
Finland	Helsinki	Finnish	a Finn
France	Paris	French	a Frenchman (or woman)
Germany	Berlin	German	a German

Country	Capital	Language	A person
Ghana	Accra	English	a Ghanaian
Greece	Athens	Greek	a Greek
Grenada	St George's	English	a Grenadian
Holland	Amsterdam	Dutch	a Dutchman (or woman)
Hungary	Budapest	Hungarian	a Hungarian
India	New Delhi	Hindi	an Indian
Indonesia	Jakarta	Bahasa Indonesian	an Indonesian
Iran	Teheran	Farsi	an Iranian
Iraq	Baghdad	Arabic	Iraqi
Ireland (Eire)	Dublin	Irish, English	an Irishman (or woman)
Israel	Jerusalem	Hebrew, Arabic	an Israeli
Italy	Rome	Italian	an Italian
Jamaica	Kingston	English	a Jamaican
Japan	Tokyo	Japanese	a Japanese (man or woman)
Jordan	Amman	Arabic	a Jordanian
Kenya	Nairobi	Kiswahili	a Kenyan
Liberia	Monrovia	English	a Liberian
Libya	Tripoli	Arabic	a Libyan
Malaysia	Kuala Lumpur	Bahasa, Malaysia	a Malaysian
Malta	Valletta	English	a Maltese (man or woman)
Mauritius	Port Louis	English, French	a Mauritian
Mexico	Mexico City	Spanish	a Mexican
Morocco	Rabat	Arabic	a Moroccan
New Zealand	Wellington	English	a New Zealander
Nigeria	Lagos	English	a Nigerian
Norway	Oslo	Norwegian	a Norwegian

Country	Capital	Language	A person
Pakistan	Islamabad	Urdu	a Pakistani
Peru	Lima	Spanish	a Peruvian
Philippines	Manila	Tagalog, Cebuano	a Filipino (m) a Filipina (f)
Poland	Warsaw	Polish	a Pole
Portugal	Lisbon	Portuguese	a Portuguese
Romania	Bucharest	Romanian	a Romanian
Russia	Moscow	Russian	a Russian
Saudi (Arabia)	Riyadh	Arabic	a Saudi (Arabian)
Singapore	Singapore City	Mandarin Chinese, English, Malay, Tamil	a Singaporean
Spain	Madrid	Spanish	a Spaniard
Sri Lanka	Colombo	Sinhala, Tamil	a Sri Lankan
Sudan	Khartoum	Arabic	a Sudanese
Sweden	Stockholm	Swedish	a Swede
Switzerland	Berne	French, German, Italian	a Swiss
Syria	Damascus	Arabic	a Syrian
Thailand	Bangkok	Thai	a Thai
Trinidad and Tobago	Port of Spain	English	a Trinidadian
Turkey	Ankara	Turkish	a Turk
Uganda	Kampala	English	a Ugandan
United Kingdom	London	English	a citizen of the UK
United States of America	Washington DC	English	an American
Vietnam	Hanoi	Vietnamese	a Vietnamese
Zambia	Lusaka	English	a Zambian
Zimbabwe	Harare	English	a Zimbabwean

Exercise 2

What do we call a person from each of these countries?

1 Poland *3* Sweden *5* Switzerland *7* Peru

2 Denmark *4* Pakistan *6* Singapore *8* Thailand

Exercise 3

What is the nationality of somebody who was born in these places?

1 Budapest *3* Damascus *5* Port of Spain *7* Athens

2 Rome *4* Kampala *6* Madrid *8* Helsinki

29 Crime and the Police

1 Crime and Criminals	*2* The Police	*3* In Court

Check that you understand the following:

People

a criminal	a suspect	a thief	an accomplice
a habitual criminal	the accused	a robber	a pickpocket
a first offender	a convict	a burglar	a gangster

Crimes

burglary	shop-lifting	homicide	fraud	forgery
theft	kidnapping	murder	arson	looting
robbery	bribery	manslaughter	assault	extortion
perjury	blackmail	drug trafficking	counterfeiting	

29.1 The Police

a policeman	a police constable	a sergeant	handcuffs
a policewoman	a police officer	an inspector	a baton
on the beat	a detective	a superintendent	to arrest

Exercise 1

Complete these sentences by putting in words from page 139.

1 A male or female police officer who always works in civilian clothes is probably a _____

2 A police _____ usually has three stripes on his arm or shoulder.

3 A policeman can put _____ on the wrists of a suspect to stop him from fighting or running away easily.

4 A person who breaks into a person's home to steal things is a _____

5 If somebody signs another person's name on a cheque and then cashes it, he may be charged with _____ .

6 A _____ uses force when he commits a crime but a _____ does not.

7 A _____ is a weapon which police officers usually carry.

8 If somebody swears to tell the truth in a court but then tells lies, he can be charged with committing _____ .

9 A superintendent is higher in rank that an _____ .

10 Mr X was drunk while he was driving his car. He knocked down and killed cyclist, so he was charged with _____ and not with murder.

29.2 In Court

a witness	a lawyer	a judge	evidence
an eye-witness	a solicitor	a jury	an alibi
a defendant	a barrister	innocent	on probation
a plaintiff	an attorney	guilty	released on bail
a prosecutor	a magistrate	acquitted	remanded in custody
a life sentence	a suspended sentence	on probation	juvenile crimes

Exercise 2

Complete these sentences by putting in words from the above list.

1 An _____ is somebody who can describe what he or she saw.

2 The _____ is somebody who appears in court and is accused of having broken the law.

3 _____ are crimes committed by young people.

4 If a guilty person is put _____ he will not go to prison but he must report to a probation officer regularly.

5 A solicitor is a ————— and so is an attorney.

6 When somebody is given a _____ , he does not stay in prison for the rest of his life but is often released after eight to twelve years.

7 If somebody is accused of a crime which he has not committed, he will probably say that he is _____ and plead not _____ at his trial.

8 An _____ is proof that you were somewhere else when a crime was committed.

9 The _____ is the person who says what the sentence will be when an accused person is found guilty.

10 When somebody is accused of a crime, a _____ will produce _____ to show that the person is _____ and not innocent.

30 Derivations

30.1 Latin

Latin is the language used by Julius Caesar and the Romans at least
2000 years ago. The Roman Empire included all Mediterranean
countries including Italy, France, Spain and Greece. Latin became
the language of the Roman Catholic Church and was used by
scholars in Europe for hundreds of years. By using Latin, a Greek
scholar could communicate with scholars throughout Europe –
because they all used Latin.

In modern times, many Latin words are still used by doctors and
nurses, biologists, lawyers, Roman Catholic priests and nuns,
archaeologists, zoologists and other scientists. We saw in Chapter 15
that a.m., p.m., e.g., etc. and i.e. are abbreviations of Latin words.

30.2 English words from Latin words

Many English words have come from Latin (and some from
German, French and Greek).

Latin word	English words formed from it
pedes (feet)	pedestrian, pedal, pedestal, impede (prevent from doing something), biped (with two feet), tripod, quadruped, octopus
medicus (doctor)	medicine, medical, remedy
amo (love)	amateur (somebody who does something for the love of it and not for money), amiable, amicable, amorous, enemy (not loved)

Exercise 1

Can you think of any modern English words made from these Latin
words?

The meaning of the Latin words is given in brackets.

1 labor (work)	*5* curro (run)	*9* navis (ship)
2 ager (field)	*6* liber (book)	*10* servus (slave)
3 culto (dig)	*7* milites (soldiers)	*11* verto (turn)
4 ager + culto	*8* porto (carry	*12* scio (know)

31 Diminutives and the Young

1 Diminutives	2 Young animals

31.1 Diminutives

-en   kitten, chicken, maiden

-ette   kitchenette, cigarette, serviette

-let   leaflet, booklet, pamphlet, starlet, islet, eaglet, piglet

-ling   duckling, darling (a little dear), seedling, gosling

31.2 Young animals

adult	young	adult	young	adult	young
bear	cub	fox	cub	pig	piglet
butterfly⎫ moth ⎭	caterpillar	frog	tadpole	rabbit	baby, rabbit
cat	kitten	goat	kid	seal	pup
cow	calf	goose	gosling	sheep	lamb
deer	fawn	hen	chick	swan	cygnet
dog	puppy	human	child	tiger	cub
duck	duckling	leopard	cub	toad	tadpole
eagle	eaglet	lion	cub	whale	calf
elephant	calf	mare	*foal		
		owl	owlet		

Warning It is not worth learning uncommon names. For example, the young of a hare is a leveret but most people have never seen a hare and would not understand what a 'leveret' is, so there is no point in using the word.

If you cannot remember the name of a young animal, you can always use 'baby', e.g. "We saw a leopard with three baby leopards."

*The young of a horse or an ass is called a foal. A male foal is called a colt. A female foal is called a filly.

32 Flowers, Herbs and Spices and Gardening Tools

1 Flowers	*2* Herbs and Spices *3* Gardening Tools

32.1 Flowers

How many of these flowers have you seen? Their common names are in brackets.

amaranthus (Love-lies-bleeding)

antirrhinum (Snapdragon)

aster

balsam (touch-me-not)

begonia

bluebell

canna (Indian shot)

carnation

chrysanthemum

crocus

daffodil

dahlia

daisy

dandelion (a weed)

digitalis (foxglove)

fuchsia

geranium

gladiolus

gypsophila (Baby's Breath)

helianthus (Sunflower)

hibiscus

honeysuckle

hyacinth

impatiens (Busy Lizzie)

larkspur (Delphinium)

lavatera (mallow)

lilac

lily

lupin

marigold

mimulus (Monkey Flower)

myosotis (Forget-me-not)

narcissus

nasturtium

nicotiana (Tobacco Plant)

nigella (Love-in-a-mist)

orchid

pansy

petunia

pink

polyanthus

poppy

primula (Primrose)

rhododendron

rose

salvia	thunbergia (Black-eyed Susan)
schizanthus (Poor Man's Orchid)	verbena
snowdrop	viola
stock	violet
sunflower	wallflower
sweet pea	zinnia
sweet william	

32.2 Herbs and Spices

Have you ever eaten any of these herbs and spices? Can you say what it tastes or smells like?

basil	ginger	nutmeg	rosemary
chilli	horseradish	paprika	sage
cloves	mint	parsley	thyme
garlic	mustard	peppermint	vanilla

Exercise 1

Answer these questions about the flowers in 32.1 and the herbs and spices in 32.2.

1 What colour is mustard when it is eaten?

2 Which herb/spice is often used to flavour ice-cream?

3 Which herb/spice is often used to flavour chewing-gum?

4 Which of these is NOT hot to eat: chilli, ginger, mint, horseradish, mustard?

5 When we say 'thyme', which consonant is silent?

6 Which flower may grow bigger than the others and have a flower larger than the others?

7 Name THREE flowers which grow from bulbs.

8 What colour is the centre of a thunbergia?

9 What colour do you think snowdrops usually are?

10 Which flower was once called 'the eye of the day'?

32.3 Gardening Tools

Do you know what these things are used for?

hoe	fork	secateurs	watering-can	shovel
bin	rake	chain-saw	strimmer	shears
saw	pliers	pickaxe	scissors	scythe
hose	spade	lawn-mower	trowel	sieve

Exercise 2

Put in the missing words.

1 We can use a _____ to separate stones from earth.

2 A gardener often uses a _____ to kill weeds.

3 A _____ is a curved knife or blade and is used to cut long grass.

4 If the soil is very hard, a gardener may have to use a _____ to break it up.

5 A _____ is a small tool used to dig up something.

6 A _____ uses a strong nylon thread to cut grass and weeds.

7 We can put a small amount of water on plants with a _____ or a larger amount by using a _____ .

8 A gardener often uses _____ or a pair of _____ to cut off dead flowers.

33 Flying

Check that you know these words:

an aeroplane	to depart
an airplane	to arrive
a plane	to taxi
a helicopter	to cruise
a (jumbo) jet	a runway
a hot-air balloon	a pilot
a microlite	a co-pilot
a glider	a flight engineer
landing gear	a cabin attendant
wings	a steward
engines	a stewardess
the port side	an air hostess
the starboard side	radar
turbulence	a hangar
a seat-belt	the Control Tower
a life-jacket	Air Traffic Controllers
an oxygen mask	the check-in counter
the galley	the ground staff
an aisle	an engineer/a mechanic
a chute	
a life raft	
to land	
to take off	

the flight crew on the flight deck: a pilot, a co-pilot, a flight engineer

the cabin crew: a cabin attendant, a steward, a stewardess, an air hostess

34 Food (including Fruit and Vegetables)

Check that you understand the following:

cereal	biscuit	sugar	chutney	cocoa
porridge	pie	jam	sauce	milk
bread	pudding	marmalade	pickles	(shake)
roll	dessert	butter	mustard	tea
bun	sago	margarine	vinegar	coffee
sandwich	jelly	sandwich spread	olive oil	orange juice
cake	tapioca	cheese	salad dressing	lemonade
pancake	(creamed) rice	coleslaw	water	lemon squash
flan	custard	salad	mineral water	Coca Cola
doughnut	ice-cream	tomato ketchup	chocolate	
	fudge			

Fruit

apple	blackcurrant	grapefruit	nectarine
pomegranate	apricot	redcurrant	greengage
orange	pomelo	avocado	white currant
guava	passion fruit	raspberry	banana
damson	lemon	peach	star fruit
blueberry	durian	loganberry	pear
strawberry	cherry	gooseberry	mango
pineapple	wine berry	coconut	grape

Vegetables

asparagus	cabbage	garlic	parsnip	sprouts
aubergine	carrot	leek	pea	swedes
(broad) beans	cauliflower	lettuce	pepper	tomatoes
(long) beans	celery	marrow	potato	turnips
beetroot	corn(sweet)	onion	radish	
broccoli	cucumber	parsley	spring onion	

35 Geography

Check that you know the meaning of these words:

stream	rain	equator	ridge	grass
river	rainfall	equatorial	gradient	bushes
source	climate	mineral	relief	desert
current	cloud	forest	marsh	sand
waterfall	fog	reservoir	swamp	oasis
whirlpool	mist	compass	glacier	volcano
tributary	breeze	map	cape	crater
pond	wind	atlas	bay	lava
lake	storm	population	peninsula	erupt (v)
sea	gale	migrate	plain	earthquake
ocean	hurricane	immigration	prairie	farming
bay	typhoon	emigration	steppe	mining
beach	lightning	imports	contours	manufac-turing
pebbles	thunder	exports	temperature	fishing
shingle	hail	hill	urban	tropical
reef	sleet	slope	rural	coral
snow	valley	avalanche	plateau	vegetation
atoll	frost	mountain	landslide	sand dune
temperate	range	erosion	under-growth	

Put in suitable words from the lists above.

1 In the Far East, a monsoon storm is called a hurricane. In the Caribbean it is called a _____ and it can cause a great deal of damage.

2 Smooth stones on a beach are known as _____ Small ones are called _____ .

3 We might expect to see a _____ between two mountains.

4 Sometimes a _____ forms where two currents meet. It can pull small vessels down below the surface.

5 When there is an _____ , the ground may open, and buildings may slide into a crack in the ground.

6 When a _____ erupts, ashes and _____ may come out.

7 A _____ is like a river of ice. It carries rocks and boulders along.

8 It is much hotter in countries near the _____ than in temperate regions.

9 A small river which flows into a bigger one is called a _____ .

10 In a _____ , nomads would go to an _____ to find water for themselves and their animals.

36 Health and Hospitals

People		Places	Departments
a patient	a doctor	a clinic	Casualty
a nurse	a physician	a hospital	X-ray
a staff nurse	a surgeon	a ward	Out-patients
a ward sister	a radiologist	ambulance	Intensive Care
a matron	a physiotherapist	the reception desk	ENT (ear, nose, throat)
a midwife	an anaesthetist	a sanatorium	Children's
a dispenser	a consultant	a convalescent home	Maternity
a pharmacist	an intern	an operating theatre	Geriatric
a dietician	a nursing aid	the pharmacy	Contagious diseases
a porter	a ward orderly	a waiting-room	Pathology

Ill health, illnesses and diseases

a cold	migraine	mumps	asthma	tonsillitis
a fever	a cough	measles	malaria	appendicitis
the flu	a swollen ...	German measles	diarrhoea	malnutrition
influenza	a broken ...	chicken-pox	cancer	indigestion
a headache	a rash	bronchitis	an allergy	a heart attack
arthritis	acne	epilepsy	a stroke	angina
glaucoma	choking	rheumatism	tuberculosis	blindness

Other words related to health and hospitals

medicine	an injury	temperature	a bandage
poison	pills	a wound	a thermometer
plaster	antidote	an injection	an accident
contagious	splints	a stretcher	a dose
an emergency	infectious	crutches	a stethoscope
a cure	treatment	antiseptic	a sling
a wheelchair	anaesthetics	transfusion	antibiotic
a microscope	disabled	bacteria	a virus
a dressing	First Aid	Red Cross	

37 At Home

Parts of a home

the attic	the hall	the basement
the kitchen	the bathroom	the living-room
a bedroom	the lounge	the cellar
reception rooms	the dining-room	a toilet

Furniture

armchair	desk	rug
settee/sofa	bed	drawer
sheet	camp-bed	dresser
shelf	carpet	duvet
sideboard	chest of drawers	eider-down
stool	coffee table	mat
table	curtains	mattress
wardrobe	cushion	pillow

In the kitchen

Crockery	Cutlery		
basin	fork	fish knife	dessert spoon
bowl	cake fork	steak knife	soup spoon
cup	grater	rolling-pin	tin-opener
dish	knife	spoon	
plate	bread knife	teaspoon	
saucer	carving knife	tablespoon	

Ways of cooking

boil	roast
fry	steam
grill	stew

Things used in a kitchen

baking tins	oven
colander	refrigerator
dish-washer	saucepan
frying-pan	toaster
kettle	wok
microwave	

38 Homonyms and Homophones

Homonyms are words which have the same spelling and sound but have different origins and meanings, e.g.

a I'm tired. I think I'll have a rest.

b There are only two oranges left. Who took the rest of them?

c Our school is going to have a fun fair next week to raise funds for a new science block.

d We all agreed that the decision of the referee was quite fair.

Homophones are words which have the same sound when we say them but are spelt differently and have different meanings, e.g.

a Wait for us! We won't be long.

b What do you think the weight of this sack is?

c Write your name and address here.

d Turn right when you reach the traffic lights.

Exercise 1

In each sentence, find a word which we can use with a different meaning.
Make up a short sentence containing the word with its different meaning.
Do NOT change the spelling of the word.

1 Mary Brown was the sole survivor of the shipwreck.

2 Most athletes train regularly to keep in good condition.

3 Did you watch the football match on television yesterday?

4 "Sorry we're late. We got caught in a traffic jam."

5 Both of the opening batsmen were out for a duck.

6 That bird is a swallow; it flies near the ground and catches insects.

7 Mrs King had a stern look on her face when she entered the room.

Vocabulary

8 Is this key yours or mine?

9 Peter swam across the river and climbed up the bank on the other side.

10 The next bus for Kingston leaves in ten minutes' time.

Exercise 2

Use the following words correctly in your own sentences.

1 wait	*3* steal	*5* fair	*7* fort	*9* brake
2 weight	*4* steel	*6* fare	*8* fought	*10* break

Check that you understand the meaning of the words below.

air	heir	currant	current
allowed	aloud	dear	deer
ate	eight	die	dye
bail	bale	draft	draught
bare	bear	ewe	yew, you
beach	beech	faint	feint
beat	beet	fair	fare
berth	birth	fate	fete
blew	blue	feat	feet
board	bored	find	fined
bough	bow	fir	fur
boy	buoy	flea	flee
brake	break	flour	flower
buy	by	for	four
ceiling	sealing	foul	fowl
cell	sell	gait	gate
cellar	seller	gilt	guilt
cent	sent, scent	gnaw	nor
cereal	serial	grate	great
cheap	cheep	groan	grown
check	cheque	hail	hale

154

hair	hare	one	won
hall	haul	pail	pale
heal	heel	pain	pane
hear	here	pair	pear
heard	herd	pause	paws
higher	hire	peace	piece
him	hymn	peal	peel
hoard	horde	pedal	peddle
hole	whole	peer	pier
holy	wholly	place	plaice
hour	our	plain	plane
idle	idol	pore	pour
key	quay	practice	practise
knew	new	praise	prays
knight	night	pray	prey
knot	not	principle	principal
know	no	prophet	profit
knows	nose	rain	rein
leak	leek	raise	rays
led	lead	rap	wrap
lessen	lesson	read	reed
loan	lone	read	red
made	maid	real	reel
mail	male	right	write
main	mane	ring	wring
mare	mayor	road	road
meat	meet	role	roll
medal	meddle	root	route
miner	minor	rose	rows
missed	mist	sail	sale
moor	more	scene	seen
muscle	mussel	scent	cent, sent
none	nun	sea	see
oar	or	seam	seem

155

sew	so	threw	through
shore	sure	throne	thrown
sight	site	tide	tied
soar	sore	time	thyme
sole	soul	tire	tyre
son	sun	to	two
stair	stare	toe	tow
stake	steak	told	tolled
stationary	stationery	vain	vein
steal	steel	vale	veil
stile	style	waist	waste
storey	story	wait	weight
straight	strait	war	wore
suite	sweet	weak	week
tail	tale	weather	whether
their	there	wood	would

Exercise 3

Choose the correct words from the brackets.

1 Susan can't remember (where, wear) she left her watch.

2 She doesn't know (whether, weather) she left it at school or (knot, not).

3 It looks as if the final will take (plaice, place) on Saturday (weak, week).

4 If (their, there) is an express bus to the city, how much is the (fair, fare)?

5 It is dangerous to swim (here, hear) because of the strong (currants, currents).

6 Mr King just managed to avoid hitting a (stationary, stationery) vehicle yesterday.

7 It was difficult for him to see clearly because of the (missed, mist).

8 There's quite a (draft, draught) coming under that door.

9 John always likes to walk about with (bare, bear) feet.

10 We need a (knew, new) (pain, pane) of glass in this window.

Exercise 4

Choose the best words to put in the sentences.

1 A hen is a type of _____

    A fool   B foul   C fowl   D paltry

2 We _____ the _____ of an accident on our way to school.

    A past _____ scene   C passed _____ scenery
    B past _____ scenery   D passed _____ scene

3 Don't throw those bags away. Remember the old saying:
    " _____ not, want _____ "

    A waste _____ not   C waist _____ knot
    B waste _____ knot   D waist _____ not

4 Yesterday one of our _____ fell over a _____ and broke a _____

    A labours _____ pale   C labours _____ pale
           _____ leg   _____ neck
    B neighbours _____ pail   D neighbours _____
           _____ neck   pail _____ leg

5 Susan has a cut on her left _____ but it will soon _____

    A heel _____ hell   C heal _____ heel
    B heal _____ heal   D heel _____ heal

6 If you go on a _____ you may feel sea-sick.

    A cruise   C clues
    B crews   D crows

7 How many _____ are _____ in this building?

    A floors _____ their   C storeys _____ there
    B stories _____ their   D story _____ there

8 The _____ in the _____ needs to be repaired.

    A ceiling _____ cellar   C sealing _____ seller
    B sealing _____ cellar   D cieling _____ seller

39 Hotels and Tourism

Check that you understand these words and can spell them correctly.

People

a tourist	the manager	a receptionist	a security guard
a waiter	the duty manager	a bell-boy	a hotel detective
a chef	the house-keeper	a cashier	a maintenance man
a guest	a maid	a porter	a bar-tender
a guide	a tout	a telephone operator	

Activities and Facilities

to check in/out	to make a reservation	to page somebody
to register	to book a room/table	to complain
room service	a four-course dinner	a buffet
a lift/an elevator	a service charge	a tip
a credit card	a bill (check)	a traveller's cheque

Places

the reception desk	a parking lot	a restaurant
the lounge/foyer	a single/double room	a coffee shop
a rest room	adjoining rooms	a swimming-pool
a toilet/W.C.	a suite	a shopping arcade
a beauty salon	a night-club	a discotheque

Travel

a scheduled flight	the scheduled departure time
a charter(ed) flight	estimated time of arrival (ETA)
a single (one way) ticket	go through Immigration and the Customs
a return (round trip) ticket	
economy/coach class	the green/red channel (for Customs)
business class	
first class	to board a plane (boarding pass)
a health certificate	a passport a refund
cabin luggage	a visa a security check
a baggage allowance	in transit a re-entry permit

40 Occupations

Check that you know what the following people do. Notice that where 'man' is used in an occupation, the same work can usually be done by a woman.

accountant	bouncer	decorator
actor	bricklayer	dental assistant
actress	bus-driver	dental hygienist
aeroplane pilot	butcher	dentist
aeroplane engineer	cabinet-maker	designer
aeroplane cabin attendant	caddie (golf)	detective
	cameraman	doctor
airman (RAF)	caretaker	draper
air traffic controller	carpenter	draughtsman
announcer	cashier	dress designer
archaeologist	chauffeur	driving instructor
architect	check-out person	dustman
artist	chef	electrician
commercial artist	chemist	electronics technician
assessor	child care assistant	

athlete	fireman	lawyer
auctioneer	fisherman	lecturer
author(ess)	fishmonger	legal assistant
bailiff	florist	librarian
bank manager(ess)	football player	library assistant
barber	fruit seller	locksmith
barman	funeral director	lorry-driver
barrister	gamekeeper	magistrate
beautician	garbageman	maid
biologist	gardener	make-up artist
blacksmith	gas engineer	manicurist
bodyguard	glazier	mason
bookkeeper	goldsmith	matron
chiropodist	golfer	mechanic
cleaner	governess	merchant marine officer
clerk	greengrocer	
clothier	grocer	meter reader
clown	hairdresser	midwife
coastguard	health inspector	miner
computer operator	heating engineer	minister
conductor	herbalist	model
cook	horticulturist	musician
counsellor	Immigration officer	nanny
Customs officer	interior decorator	naval officer
data preparation operator	ironmonger	navvy
	janitor	newsagent
engineer (civil, electrical or mechanical)	jeweller	novelist
	jockey	nurse
farmer	joiner	nursing assistant
farm labourer	journalist	optician
farrier	judge	paralegal
financial services officer	laboratory technician	paramedic
		pawnbroker
	landscape gardener	

pest control operator	roofer	stevedore
pharmacist	saddler	steward(ess) stoker
photographer	sailor	street sweeper
physician	sales person	surgeon
pilot	scientific officer	surveyor
plasterer	scientist	tailor
plumber	script writer	taxation officer
police officer	sculptor	teacher
porter	secretary	telephone operator
postman	security guard	teller
presenter (TV)	service engineer	tennis-player
prison officer	shepherd	tourist guide
probation officer	shoe repairer	traffic warden
professor	shop assistant	train-driver
programmer	signalman	travel agent
public relations officer	singer	typist
quality controller	social worker	undertaker
radiographer	soldier	upholsterer
radiologist	solicitor	veterinary surgeon
receptionist	stacker	waiter-waitress
referee	stationer	watch repairer
reporter	steeplejack	
	stenographer	

Exercise 1

Do you know of any occupations which are not given on the previous pages? If so, what are they?

Exercise 2

Which of the people on the previous pages does these things?

1 delivers the mail

2 goes to people's homes to destroy ants and cockroaches

3 throws people out of a night-club if they cause trouble

 4 keeps the roads clean in a town

 5 can arrange an overseas holiday for customers

 6 writes the story for a television film or play

 7 lends money to people if they take jewellery and valuable objects to him

 8 says "For the third and last time ... going, going, gone!"

 9 says "Fasten your seat belts and prepare for landing, please."

 10 says "You will go to prison for three years."

Exercise 3

Which of the people on the previous pages might do these things?

 1 advises women on how to look more beautiful

 2 repairs cars (and often other machines)

 3 repairs a leaking pipe

 4 travels in an ambulance and gives medical assistance

 5 puts goods on shelves and stacks in a supermarket

 6 arranges a funeral when somebody dies

 7 replaces broken windows

 8 drives a car for his or her employer and often wears a uniform

 9 receives guests when they come to register at a hotel

 10 decides whether or not a visitor to a country can be admitted

Exercise 4

Which of the people on the previous pages might use these things?

 1 scissors, a comb and perhaps a razor

 2 paints and an easel

 3 a stethoscope and a thermometer

 4 a tape measure, chalk and scissors

 5 a baton, handcuffs and sometimes a gun

 6 a microphone

 7 mortar and a trowel

 8 a plane, a chisel and a saw

 9 a helmet, an axe and breathing apparatus

 10 his feet, his head, his chest but never his hands

41 Odd One Out

In each exercise, find the word which does not belong with others in the same line.

Exercise 1

1 lion, leopard, bear, vulture, elephant, rhinoceros, hippopotamus

2 orange, plum, pear, banana, nectarine, papaya, potato, raspberry

3 van, bicycle, lorry, car, station-wagon, truck, coach, bus

4 woman, actress, waitress, aunt, daughter, baby, niece, grand-mother, sister

5 clay, copper, zinc, brass, tin, lead, steel, aluminium, platinum, silver

6 dollar, pound, kilogram, yen, mark, franc, lira, baht, rand, peseta, rupee

7 Trinidad, St Lucia, Tobago, Jamaica, Mauritius, Antigua, Grenada, St Vincent

8 Tanzania, Somalia, Namibia, Nigeria, Algeria, Paraguay, Mozambique, Angola

9 violin, trumpet, drum, barrel, cello, flute, harp, piano, clarinet, organ

10 brakes, spokes, pedals, chain, gears, wheels, flame, saddle, carrier

Exercise 2

1 chat, tell, speak, say, request, demand, talk, listen, suggest, remark

2 dog, cat, horse, ox, hen, cow, duck, goose, buffalo, elephant, tiger

3 yard, garden, kilometre, mile, foot, metre, centimetre, inch, furlong

4 freezing, very cold, cold, cool, warm, frozen, hot, very hot, boiling

5 minute, tiny, quite small, small, medium-size, quite big, fat, huge

6 first, second, minute, hour, day, week, month, year, decade, century

7 limp, hobble, saunter, walk, stand, run, sprint, trot, gallop, canter

8 ear, hair, scalp, forehead, eyelash, eyebrow, throat, teeth, tongue, lips

9 friendly, helpful, amiable, pleasant, cheerful, hostile, generous, kind

10 diamond, gold, ruby, sapphire, emerald, jade, opal, pearl, aquamarine

Exercise 3

1 Susan, Margaret, Ann, Joan, Barbara, Elizabeth, Carolyn, Arthur, Diana

2 mallet, hammer, finger, nail, screw, chisel, plane, drill, vice, clamp

3 Atlantic, Mediterranean, Pacific, Indian, Arctic, Antarctic

4 July, November, February, December, Sunday, March, August, May, April

5 vinegar, sauce, kerosene, paraffin, water, bread, tea, coffee, petrol

6 theft, robbery, assault, forgery, burglary, prison, kidnapping

7 Spaniard, New Zealander, Thai, Pole, Japanese, British, Jamaican

8 four, nine, sixteen, twenty-five, thirty-six, forty-nine, fifty-eight

42 Phrasal Verbs

Phrasal verbs such as put up, come across and get over are very common in English, especially in speech. Sometimes a phrasal verb can have more than one meaning, e.g.

put up

= raise	*1* Mary knew the answer so she put up her hand.
= increase	*2* Taxi-drivers have just put up their fares.
= build	*3* Some workmen have just put up three houses in three weeks.
= stay	*4* Uncle sometimes puts up at a friend's home in London.
= provide accommodation	*5* We can put up two members of the visiting soccer team for a fortnight.
= provide	*6* Ms King has put up $1000 to buy prizes for the best four pupils.
= get somebody to do something	*7* Who put you up to this?

In each of the following exercises, choose the right explanation of the words in bold type.

Exercise 1

1 When the strikers asked for a pay increase of 10%, the manager refused to consider it. Two weeks later, he **backed down** and offered an increase of 8%.

    A ran away   B gave way   C became angry   D fell over

2 You can **bank on** us to support you at the meeting.

    A object to   B agree with   C rely on   D stand on

3 The workmen are **behind** with the repairs to the roof.

A late in finishing   C hiding away
B unwilling to start   D getting on quickly

4 What are those boys talking about? I wonder what they're **up to**.

A standing on   C planning to do
B climbing up   D arguing about

5 Go and help Mary to **blow up** the balloons for the party.

A put air into   C hang up
B explode   D go and buy

6 Terrorists have threatened to **blow up** an important pipe line.

A expand   C insert air into
B take control of   D damage by an explosion

7 World War II **broke out** in 1939.

A finished   C became worse
B started   D was cancelled

8 Uncle said he will probably **call round** at about seven o'clock this evening.

A telephone   C expect you to visit him
B shout across to   D come and see (you)

9 The scheme is a good one but don't get **carried away** by it. It hasn't been approved yet.

A overcome by excitement   C forced to feel ill
B too worried   D eager to oppose something

10 Yes, your plan looks quite good. **Carry on** with it.

A Take it away   C Agree
B Continue   D Change it again

Exercise 2

1 What did the injured man say when he **came to**?

A arrived   C reached us
B visited   D recovered consciousness

2 Sgt Johnson suspects that Peter is **covering up** for a friend.

A falsely accusing   C hiding behind
B lying to protect   D trying to find

3 Mary was **cut off** while she was talking to Susan on the phone.

A disconnected   C accidentally hurt
B injured   D very surprised

4 Did your sister **get through** her driving test yesterday?

A take   C fail
B pass   D arrive at

5 How does he always manage to **get off** helping at home?

A stop   C suggest
B avoid   D quickly complete

6 Do you think she will **get over** her illness soon?

A forget about   C find out about
B stop worrying about   D recover from

7 I hope the meat hasn't **gone off** because of the heat.

A become bad   C been eaten
B disappeared   D increased in price

8 (On the telephone) "Please **hang on** a minute."

A stay on the line and wait   C don't phone
B listen and take notes   D stop talking

9 Ann **jumped at** the opportunity to study overseas.

A strongly object to   C quickly accepted
B refused to accept   D decided to think over

10 Although we **let off** fireworks in the school grounds, the head-master **let us off** with a scolding.

A burnt _____ punished   C ignited _____ exploded
B found _____ forgave   D exploded _____ released

Exercise 3

Choose the right words to be put in the following sentences.

1 If robbers give _____ to the police, they surrender.

A in   B out   C away   D down

2 When passengers arrive from a foreign country, Customs officers may decide to go _____ their luggage to look for drugs or other things.

A at   B into   C through   D across

3 Line _____ if you are waiting to buy tickets.

    A about   B straight   C along   D up

4 Would you mind looking _____ this letter for me? Tell me if you find any mistakes in it.

    A through   B about   C to   D for

5 Can you make _____ what this letter is? Is it an 'm' or a 'u'?

    A up   B out   C off   D over

6 We were sorry to hear that Mary's grandfather passed _____ during the night.

    A along   B off   C up   D away

7 When Mary's old dog could no longer walk, she asked a vet to put it _____

    A off   B out   C over   D down

8 Don't leave your books on the table. Put them _____

    A off   B away   C down   D out

9 Why don't you ring Susan _____ and find out how her brother is?

    A down   B up   C off   D out

10 The Government is going to round _____ stray dogs and put them in kennels.

    A across   B down   C out   D up

43 Places

Exercise 1

Match the following places with the people or things we can see inside them.

1 an aquarium	pictures
2 an arcade	aeroplanes
3 a barracks	bees
4 a cemetery	guests
5 a clinic	graves
6 a gallery	patients
7 a hangar	fish
8 a hive	science
9 a hotel	apparatus
10 a laboratory	shops
	soldiers

11 a kennel	shops
12 a library	wild animals
13 a mall	clothes
14 a marina	a dog
15 a mortuary	fruit trees
16 an orchard	books
17 a ring	horses
18 stables	yachts
19 a wardrobe	boxers
20 a zoo	dead bodies

Exercise 2

Match the following places with the descriptions of what may happen in them.

1 a mosque	This is where oil can be treated to produce petrol.
2 a motel	You might see young children or young plants or trees here.
3 a museum	
4 a nursery	You might see a prisoner, or a ship being repaired here.
5 a warehouse	This is a good place for repairing machines.
6 a distillery	You can store huge quantities of grain here.
7 a refinery	This is where Muslims pray.
8 a dock	You can often see old things in this place.
9 a granary	Alcohol or salt water can be treated and changed here.
10 a workshop	If you want to store goods, this is the right place for you.
	Guests at this place arrive in their own cars.

169

Exercise 3

Match the places with the descriptions.

1 a depot	This large place is for sporting events; many spectators can watch.
2 an exchange	Many buses, coaches or trains can be kept here.
3 a larder/ pantry	
4 an orphanage	People grow grapes and often make wine here.
5 a quarry	This is where grain can be ground to produce flour.
6 a stadium	
7 a studio	You can take a photograph or make a film in this place.
8 a vineyard	This can be for justice, badminton or tennis.
9 a court	
10 a mill	The children in this place often have no parents.

People keep food in this part of a house.

You might see telephones here or people buying and selling metals.

This is where men get large quantities of sand and gravel.

44 Prefixes

Study the prefixes and words in the following lists. Then make new words by using the given prefix with the words in square brackets [ ]. Make sure that you understand the meaning of all the words.

List 1

Prefix	Meaning	Examples
a	in(to), on, to, towards	ahead, afloat [sleep, shore]
ab	(away) from	absent, absurd, abstract [duct]
ad, a, ac, af, ag	to, towards	ascend, accident [venture]
amb(i)	both	ambiguous, ambidextrous
ante	before	antenatal (before birth) [room]
anti	against	antiseptic, anti-hunting [-aircraft]
arch	chief	archangel, arch-enemy [bishop]
auto	self	automobile, autobiography [graph]
bene	well	benevolent, benefactor [fit]
bi	two, twice	bisect, biped, biplane [cycle]
circum	around	circumference [navigate]
com, con, co	(together) with	compare, connect, co-operate [-worker]
contra	against	contrast, contraband [diction]
de	down	descend, description [part]
dia	across, through	diagnosis, diabetes [meter]
en, em	in, into, on	engulf, embrace [close]
ex, e	out (of)	exit, erupt, extract [port]
ex-	former	ex-international [-captain]
extra	outside, beyond	extramural [ordinary]
fore	before	foretell, forecast [see]

List 2

Prefix	Meaning	Examples
homo	similar, the same	homonym, homophone
in, il, im, ir	not	inedible, insufficient, incapable illegible, irregular,
dis	not	dissimilar, disagreeable
in	in, within	injection insight [side]
inter	among, between	interfere, interrupt [national]
mid	the middle of	mid-air, midway [night]
mini	small	miniskirt [cab]
mis	bad(ly), wrong(ly)	misfortune, misjudge [behave]
mono	(only) one	monosyllable, monologue, monopoly
non	not	a non-starter [sense]
oct, octa/o	eight	octopus, octagon, October (the eighth month when there were only 10 months)
out	beyond, outside	outlaw, outlive [number]
over	above, too much, outside	overcoat, overcome [work]
per	through	perspire, perforate, persecute
poly	many	polygamous [technic]
post	after	post-natal, postpone [script]
pre	before	precede (go before) [caution]
pro	for, forward	proceed, progress [motion]
quad(ri)	four	quadrilateral, quadrangle
re	again, back down	recover, readdress [turn]
semi	half	semi-conscious [circle]

List 3

sub, suc, suf, sup	under, down, lower	subway, support, suspend [marine]
super	beyond, more than	supervisor, superhuman [man]
tele	a long distance	telescope, telephone [vision]
trans	across	transfer, translate [port]
tre, tri	three	treble, tripod, tricycle [angle]
un	not	unnecessary, unable [educated]
un	(do the opposite)	unfasten, undone [tie]
un(i)	one	uniform, unicorn [verse]
under	below	underline, under hand [ground]
vice	taking the place of	vice-president [chairman]
with	against, back	withhold, withstand [draw]

45 Reference Sources

What information can we obtain from the reference sources listed below? In each exercise, match the words in the box with the information contained in the sources.

Exercise 1

album	annual	autobiography	biography	calendar
almanac	atlas	bank statement	brochure	catalogue

1 The life of a person written by himself or herself.

2 Information about a person's income and expenditure as well as his bank balance.

3 Photos or stamps or even songs and music.

4 Cartoons and stories suitable for young people.

5 A list of goods for sale and their prices.

6 Days, months and the date.

7 Information about a place or an activity, e.g. holidays, tours, etc.

8 The life of a person written by somebody else.

9 Maps and details of stars, population, flags, climate, vegetation, etc.

10 Many details about the days and months of the year, plus articles and advertisements.

Exercise 2

an auctioneer's catalogue	a pronouncing dictionary	a diary
a stamp catalogue	a directory	GCSE regulations and syllabuses
a cookery book	a telephone directory	
a dictionary	the telephone yellow pages	

1 How to say words.

2 A list of things for sale at an auction.

3 Rules about an examination and details of what students must study.

4 Lists of people and companies providing services or selling goods.

5 The meaning, spelling and pronunciation of words, plus their derivation.

6 The value of stamps.

7 People's telephone numbers and how to use the telephone.

8 The names and addresses of people and firms.

9 Recipes and advice about cooking.

10 A record of what somebody has done each day, sometimes with comments.

Exercise 3

an encyclopaedia	a horoscope	the log of a ship/plane
a guidebook	an income tax return	a school magazine
Guinness Book of Records	an insurance policy	an owner's manual
a user's manual	a newspaper	a novel

1 Details of a person's income and a claim for allowances.

2 Lists of different kinds of world records.

3 Instructions on how to use something such as a word processor.

4 Detailed information about something such as a car, and how to look after it.

5 A record of the movements of a plane or ship and of any incidents en route.

6 Articles about people, countries, science, animals, and most other things.

7 Information to show what is and is not covered by insurance against risks.

8 Advice to people, claiming to show how the stars affect their lives.

9 Information about a city, region or country, often for the use of tourists.

10 Articles by pupils, and a record of games, athletics and other achievements at school.

11 A story which is a work of fiction.

12 Advertisements, news, sports results, competitions, letters and more advertisements.

Exercise 4

a passport	a school register	a textbook
a visa	a schedule of flights	a thesaurus
a programme	a scrap-book	a timetable
an electoral register	a television guide	a zoology book

1 A list of people who can vote in a national or local election.

2 Information about a particular subject, e.g. Maths, History or Geography.

3 The picture of the owner and information about him or her, plus his nationality.

4 Permission from the government of a country to allow somebody to visit the country.

5 Cuttings from newspapers, pictures, perhaps used tickets and programmes, etc.

6 Details of future programmes on television.

7 Information about many kinds of animals.

8 Details of what will happen at an event such as a Sports Meeting or concert.

9 A list of pupils in a class and a record of their attendance.

10 Information showing which planes fly from one airport to another, when they leave and arrive, whether the flight is a direct one or not, etc.

11 Thousands of words arranged in groups and containing synonyms and antonyms.

12 Information showing what will happen at certain times (and sometimes where it will happen).

46 Science

Check that you know the meaning of the following words:

apparatus

(spring-)balance	burette	filter-paper	magnet	tongs
battery	cable	funnel	pipette	tripod
beaker	clamp	gas jar	rack	trough
bulb	crucible	gauze	rod	wire
bunsen burner	filter	litmus paper	test-tube	

texture

elastic	smooth	oily	fine	soft	hairy
springy	rough	slippery	hard	waxy	furry

shapes

circle	rectangles	sphere	oval	crescent
square	triangle	cube	oblong	S-bend

materials

china	cotton	glass	paper	rubber	wood
clay	fibre	metal	plastic	silk	asbestos
cloth	fur	nylon	porcelain	stone	aluminium

other words

acid	evaporate	contract	nuclear	compound
alkali	condense	dissolve	radiation	mixture
litmus paper	expand	react	crystal	electricity

47 Ships and the Sea

Check that you know the meaning of the following words:

In or near the sea

bay	cliff	lagoon	port	sand-fly	tide
beach	crab	lobster	prawn	sea-bed	wave
breaker	crayfish	octopus	quay	shrimp	
breakwater	current	pool	rocks	surf	

In or near a harbour

anchorage	bollard	channel	dock	pilot	warehouse
berth	buoy	derrick	godown	(inner) roads (= channel for ships)	

Parts of a ship

aerial	cabin	funnel	hull	propeller	stabilizers
anchor	crane	galley	mast	radar	starboard side
bow	deck	gangway	port-hole	rail	stern
bridge	engine	hold	port side	rudder	

Vessels

barge	container ship	junk	liner	tramp
bulk carrier	ferry	launch	sampan	trawler
cargo ship	freighter	lifeboat	speedboat	tug
catamaran	hovercraft	lighter	tanker	yacht

Warships

aircraft carrier	fleet auxiliary	mine-sweeper
battleship	frigate	submarine
cruiser	hospital ship	supply ship
destroyer	landing craft	

48 Sport and Games

Games and Sports

angling	boxing	hockey	rugby league	swimming
archery	cricket	horse racing	rugby union	squash
athletics	cycling	ice hockey	running	tennis
badminton	darts	motor racing	skating	weightlifting
baseball	fencing	netball	skiing	wrestling
basketball	football	polo	snooker	yachting
billiards	golf	rounders	soccer	
bowls	gymnastics	rowing	shooting	

Things used

arrows	cue	hurdles	puck	skates
bails	darts	javelin	racket (racquet)	skis
ball	discus	line		stick
bat	foil	net	rod	stool
baton	gloves	oars	saddle	stumps
bow	hammer	pockets	sail	tees
clubs	hook	pole	shot	weights
			shuttlecock	

People and Activities

umpire	tournament	1st base man
referee	first leg	home run
linesman	second leg	penalty
touch judge	seconds	offside
judges	twelfth man	striker
competitor	scorer	wicket-keeper
amateur	starter	bowler
professional	pitcher	
competition	catcher	

49 Suffixes

Check that you know the meaning of the following words:

Suffix	Meaning	Examples
-age	place, cost, act, condition, result	village, orphanage, anchorage, passage, marriage, damage, wreckage, stoppage, hostage, savage, carriage, postage, baggage, luggage, foliage, average
-al	belonging to or resembling	regal, royal, loyal, brutal, vertical
-ance -ence	quality or action	assistance, endurance, ignorance, attendance, silence, patience, experience, audience
-ant -ent	having a quality	assistant, attendant, ignorant, servant, silent, patient, innocent, absent
-ble, -able -ible	having a quality	breakable, enjoyable, comfortable, charitable, horrible, terrible, edible, flexible
-cide	kill(er)	homicide, insecticide, suicide, herbicide
-ee	affected by an action	employee, referee, absentee, refugee
-er, -ar, -or	one who does something	driver, swimmer, burglar, inspector
-ess	a female	actress, waitress, princess, stewardess
-fy	make	simplify, magnify, terrify, identify
-gram, -graph	written or recorded	diagram, telegram, parallelogram, photograph
-hood	state of	childhood, boyhood, falsehood, neighbourhood
-ian	a person who does something	librarian, historian, Christian, guardian
-ics	a science or system	mathematics, electronics, mechanics, politics

Exercise 1

Complete these sentences by putting in words from above.

1 The liquid in this bottle can kill insects; it is an _____ .

2 A _____ line is one which forms an angle of 90° with a horizontal one.

3 In the past, a flight attendant was called a _____ .

4 _____ means 'leaves', as found on trees or plants.

5 Most of the children in an _____ have no parents.

6 Algebra, geometry and arithmetic are parts of _____ .

7 If you work for somebody else, you are an _____ .

8 The opposite of 'guilty' is _____ .

9 A _____ has two pairs of parallel sides.

10 Scientists can use a microscope to _____ something and see what it looks like.

Suffix	Meaning	Examples
-ing	doing something	swimming, walking, singing, running
-ish	resembling, like	boyish, foolish, childish, reddish
-ism	state, condition	barbarism, heroism, favouritism, communism
-ist	person who does something	cyclist, dentist, artist, tourist
-itis	disease(d)	tonsillitis, appendicitis, arthritis, bronchitis
-less	without	careless, hopeless, harmless, useless
-ology	science or knowledge of	biology, archaeology, Egyptology, zoology
- ment	result, action or state	excitement, government, enjoyment, agreement
-meter	measuring	thermometer, barometer, odometer, pedometer
-ness	state, condition, degree	happiness, business, selfishness, politeness

-(i)ous	with the quality of	mysterious, poisonous, cautious, numerous
-phone	sound	telephone (= sound form a distance), xylophone (US zylophone), dictaphone, microphone, megaphone
-scope	seeing, watching	microscope, telescope, periscope, kaleidoscope
-ship	state, condition, quality	hardship, friendship. citizenship, membership
-tion, -sion	action or condition	attention, correction, decision collision
-y	with the quality of	healthy, dirty, greasy, greedy

Exercise 2

Complete these sentences by putting in words from above.

1 If you fasten a _____ to your leg, you can find out how far you have walked.

2 If you have a sore throat, you may be suffering from _____

3 A mechanic often has _____ and _____ hands because of his work.

4 Students of _____ study the life of animals.

5 Cobras and vipers are _____ snakes.

6 Sometimes the police use a _____ to speak to a large crowd of people.

7 Pay _____ ! Listen carefully to what I have to say!

8 The captain of a submarine uses a _____ to see what ships are on the surface above him.

9 A _____ measures temperature: a _____ measures air pressure.

10 An _____ measures the distance which a car has travelled.

11 If you are _____ and eat too much food, you may have stomach-ache later on.

12 A detective was praised for his _____ in capturing two armed men by himself.

50 Synonyms

Warning Synonyms can be dangerous.

a They may be similar in meaning but they are rarely exactly the same. For example, a girl may be happy if you say that she is slim or slender. She may NOT be pleased if you call her thin or skinny.

b Some synonyms have a similar meaning but are used in different ways, e.g.

1 John is able to walk by himself now.

2 John is capable of walking by himself now.

In the following exercises, find synonyms for the words in the boxes.

Exercise 1

above	abundant	active	abrupt	achieve	adequate
abroad	absolutely	assist	abruptly	acquire	afraid

help	accomplish	completely	sudden	overseas	obtain
over	frightened	sufficient	suddenly	plentiful	lively

Exercise 2

artificial	attempt	beginning	beneath	brave	bucket
assistance	audacious	beach	brag	breadth	buy

pail	unnatural	purchase	under	shore	bold
help	courageous	boast	width	try	start

Exercise 3

cautious	comprehend	complete	commence	courteous	candid
commend	clothes	correct	certain	cheat	choose

garments	deceive	select	polite	begin	frank
understand	careful	finish	praise	right	sure

Exercise 4

crafty	enemy	deadly	crooked	enthusiasm	discourteous
false	feeble	dawn	difficult	enormous	cultivating

keenness   cunning   impolite   fatal   weak   foe

growing   sunrise   bent   untrue   huge   hard

Exercise 5

eager	fortunately	frock	elegant	evade	espionage
fetch	frequently	futile	exactly	gaol	fracture

luckily   often   pointless   bring   keen   break

graceful   dress   precisely   prison   avoid   spying

In the following exercises, you will see TWO words at the side of each word in the box. Decide which of the two words is a synonym for the word in the box.

Exercise 6

immediately	now, instantly
mysterious	evil, strange
halted	stop, stopped
hardly	scarcely, smoothly
hinder	obstruct, disagree
illegal	legal, unlawful
imitate	copy, mock
interior	inside, into
mad	insane, upset
mariner	captain, sailor
marsh	stride, swamp
odour	perfume, smell

Exercise 7

quarrel	dispute, fight
rapidly	speedy, quickly
rare	common, seldom
refuse	decline, disagree
regret	sorry, sorrow
residence	dwelling, building
rip	open, tear
roam	wander, wonder
rough	soft, uneven
silent	noiseless, quietly
slender	thin, slim
stubborn	stupid, obstinate

51 Time

51.1 The 24-hour clock

To change from the 12-hour clock to the 24-hour clock, add 12 to the hours from 1 p.m. onwards:

12-hr clock: 9 a.m. noon 1.30 p.m. 6 p.m. 9 p.m. midnight 3. a.m.
24-hr clock: 0900   1200 1330   1800   2100   2400   0300
                                                              or 03.00

Exercise 1

Change these times to 24-hour clock times.

1 2 p.m.   *3* 7.20 p.m.   *5* half past ten   *7* 10.40 p.m.
                                     at night

2 8.30 p.m.   *4* 7.20 a.m.   *6* ten to two   *8* 5.30 p.m.
                                     in the morning

Exercise 2

Change these times to 12-hour clock times.

1 1500 hours *3* 23.59 hours *5* 21.20   *7* 0110   *9* 2000

2 06.50 hrs   *4* 2300 hours   *6* 1405   *8* 1940   *10* 22.15

51.2 Fast and Slow

fast Mary's watch is 6 minutes fast. The time on her watch is two minutes past five now.

Then the right time must be four fifty-six (or four minutes to five).

slow Peter's watch is 5 minutes slow. The time on his watch is twenty past eight now.

Then the right time must be 8.25.

Exercise 3

What is the right time in each of the following cases?
Use the 24-hr or 12-hr clock as shown below.

1 10.15 (5 minutes fast)   *2* 1900 (8 minutes fast)

3 14.58 (7 minutes slow) *4* 1303 (2 minutes slow)

5 2200 (5 minutes fast)   *6* noon (4 minutes fast)

51.3 Time Zones

This table shows the time in different parts of the world when it is noon in London.

Hawaii 2 a.m.	Guyana 8.15 a.m.	Kenya 3 p.m.	Japan 9 p.m.
California 4 a.m.	London noon	India 5 p.m.	E Australia 10 p.m.
New York ⎤ Jamaica ⎦ 7 a.m.	Nigeria 1 p.m.	Malaysia ⎤ Singapore ⎦ 7 p.m.	New Zealand midnight
Trinidad ⎤ Argentina ⎦ 8 a.m.	Zimbabwe ⎤ Zambia Malta Cyprus ⎦ 2 p.m.	Hong Kong ⎤ W Australia ⎦ 8 p.m.	

Exercise 4

1 When it is 4 p.m. in London, what is the time in these places?

 a Nigeria *b* Jamaica *c* Zambia *d* Hong Kong *e* Kenya

2 When it is noon in Malta, what is the time in these places?

 a Guyana *b* Cyprus *c* London *d* Hong Kong *e* Trinidad

52 Tests

Test I

In each case, chose the word or phrase which best shows the meaning of the underlined word.

1 The hostages were <u>released</u> when the robbers were surrounded.

  A unharmed   B injured   C set free   D taken in

2 A memorial service was held for the <u>late</u> minister.

  A deceased   B unpunctual C well known   D former

3 Each person may <u>submit</u> two entries only.

  A receive   B qualify   C consider   D send in

4 The arrest came as quite a <u>shock</u> to Mr King.

  A unpleasant surprise   C expected result

  B injury caused by electricity   D harmful act

5 The referee did not stop the game <u>despite</u> the heavy rain.

  A because of   C until

  B although there was   D since

6 The traffic had to be <u>diverted</u> as a result of a serious accident.

  A sent by another route   C stopped completely

  B slowed down considerably   D searched by policemen

7 Are you sure this old stamp is <u>genuine</u>?

  A valuable   C unused for sending a letter

  B undamaged   D what it seems to be and not a fake

8 Her story about seeing a UFO land is <u>incredible</u>.

  A very surprising   C unreliable

  B most unusual   D unbelievable

9 Mrs Brown asked the shopkeeper what <u>discount</u> he would give her.

  A advice   C free gift

  B reduction in price   D information

10 A doctor removed a <u>minute</u> piece of glass form Toyin's left eye.

A very small   C almost invisible

B very sharp   D there for a short time

11 Margaret is a very <u>amiable</u> girl.

A well-behaved B obedient   C shy   D friendly

12 Mr Brown has promised to help us but his promise was a vague one.

A unwilling   B unsuitable   C not clear   D not reliable

13 When there is a war, many of the soldiers are <u>volunteers</u>.

A men who are reluctant to fight   C men who are not physically fit

B men with previous military experience   D men who have offered to join the army

14 Mr Wilson had a thorough medical examination at our hospital.

A done quickly and not efficiently   C happening regularly every year

B done carefully and covering all areas   D involving an X-ray

15 How many of them are likely to <u>survive</u> the drought?

A live through   C be affected by

B tell us about   D die during

16 The standard of gymnastics at the Olympic Games is superb.

A greatly praised   C better than before

B very surprising   D extremely high

17 There were a good many people at the meeting.

A a lot of good   C quite a lot

B a lot of fine   D quite a lot of good

18 Do you think this dress will <u>shrink</u> if I wash it in water?

A tear   B break up   C be damaged   D get smaller

19 In an emergency, people sometimes use a church or temple as a sanctuary.

A place to get food   C place of entertainment

B shelter from danger   D means of education

Test 2

Choose the best word(s) to put in each blank space.

1 On my birthday, I had a lot of presents _____ my parents.

   A off   B at   C from   D by

2 When John won the first prize, he became _____ .

   A conceited   B big-headed   C swollen   D stuck up

3 The man had to beg for food because he was _____ .

   A penniless   B skint   C breadless   D out of the
                                                  ready

4 I am sorry for _____ you all this trouble.

   A doing   B creating   C making   D causing

5 What time are you going to _____ lunch?

   A have   B take   C eat   D consume

6 This is a film which _____ the hardships of war.

   A concerns   C is concerningwith
   B concerning with   D is concerned with

7 Mary overheard two or three boys _____ about the game.

   A chatted   B chattering   C chatting   D chattered

8 Many people believe that television will eventually _____ the cinema as a form of entertainment.

   A substitute   B extinguish   C exchange   D replace

9 Too many people wanted to enter the country so the Government decided to _____ restrictions on immigration.

   A depose   B impose   C compose   D expose

10 A person's 'arch-enemy' is his or her _____ enemy.

   A recent   B chief   C most cunning D most friendly

11 In the word 'circumnavigate', the prefix 'circum' means

_____ .

   A across   B among   C along   D around

12 Uncle has decided to sell half his cattle but _____ the others.

   A detain   B contain   C sustain   D retain

13 The suspect _____ that he is innocent.

   A persists   B insists   C resists   D desists

14 In the word 'ultra-modern', the prefix 'ultra' means _____

   A against   B before   C earlier   D towards

15 She may succeed in that type of business. _____ it is quite possible that she will fail.

   A In the other side,   C to the contrary,

   B On the other hand,   D Contrarily,

16 John asked to be _____ from the cross-country race because he was recovering from the flu.

   A accused   B pardoned   C excused   D absented

17 Did Susan _____ you the results of the tournament?

   A inform   B informed   C tell   D told

18 If you don't mind, I would _____ not play this evening.

   A prefer   B rather   C suggest   D wish

19 Mrs Wilson asked the bank manager to tell her the _____ of her account.

   A balance   B how much   C remaining   D net

Test 3

Choose the best word(s) to put in the blank space.

1 Between _____ I think he is not telling the truth.

   A I and you   C me and you

   B you and I   D you and me

2 Peter and Mary thoroughly enjoyed _____ at the picnic.

   A herself   B imself   C ourselves   D themselves

3 This is my watch. That one is _____ , Peter.

   A You're   B ours'   C your's   D yours

4 Her belt was too tight, so she _____ it.

    A losed   B lost   C loosened   D release

5 It's time you _____ your handwriting.

    A improve   B improved   C improving   D were improved

6 You need a lot of _____ when you are doing a crossword puzzle.

    A patient   B patience   C patients   D impatient

7 The film was not very _____ , so Daljit soon felt _____

    A exciting _____ boring   C excited _____ boring

    B exciting _____ bored   D excited _____ bored

8 Peter is my brother. He is _____ than I am.

    A elder   B oldest   C not as old   D older

9 A _____ man tore his shirt on our _____ fence.

    A middle-aged _____ barbed-wire

    B middle-age _____ barb-wire

    C middle-age _____ barbed-wire

    D middle-aged _____ barb-wire

10 Mr Wilson _____ objects to the plan for a new stadium.

    A very   B greatly   C too much   D strong

11 Everyone in the world _____ to lead a happy life.

    A hopes   B hope   C is hoping   D are hoping

12 She is normally very punctual and is _____ late.

    A often   B frequently   C always   D rarely

13 Collecting old and valuable stamps _____ an interesting but expensive hobby.

    A has   B is   C have   D are

14 There _____ a number of reasons why our team will probably win.

    A has   B have   C is   D are

15 The number of traffic accidents _____ fallen in the past few years.

A is   B has   C have   D are

16 You have left _____ 's' out of 'successful'.

A an   B a   C the   D (no word is needed)

17 This is _____ best chance you will get to join a group of musicians.

A a   B the   C an   D (no word is needed)

18 Uncle has just made a fine _____ of drawers for us.

A chest   B packet   C piece   D bale

19 When you go shopping, please buy two _____ of soap.

A pieces   B sticks   C rods   D bars

20 Be careful! Those two men are carrying a large _____ of glass.

A slice   B bouquet   C pane   D pain

Test 4

A In each line, underline the word that is spelt wrongly. Then write the correct spelling of the word at the end of the line.

1 successful, scenery, science, greatful, necessary   _____

2 vividly, laboratory, occured, competition, weird   _____

3 shopping, aquarium, ceiling, recieved, probably   _____

4 beautiful, until, appearance, warehouse, seperate   _____

5 dissappearance, dissolve, eager, influenza, emotion   _____

6 conquer, ninety, fourty, modern, restaurant   _____

Tests

7 skillfully, history, exhibition, fitness, audience

_____

8 satisfactory, apron, disaster, burried, punctually

_____

9 innocent, arguement, valuable, kindergarten, obeying

_____

10 hospital, compulsory, rainny, permission, development

_____

B Choose the best word(s) to be used in the blanks pace.

11 Has your cousin _____ her driving test yet?

A pass   B passed   C past

12 Was your village badly _____ by the floods?

A infected   B effected   C affected

13 We are very _____ to you for returning _____ our kitten.

A thankful _____ back   C grateful _____ (no word is needed)

B grateful _____ back

14 Please _____ me to get some rice when we go out.

A recall   B remember   C remind

15 Last week the West Indies team _____ the English team by over 300 runs.

A won   B beat   C defeat

16 John found a wallet _____ on the pavement outside Uncle's shop.

A laying   B lieing   C lying

17 Suddenly two boys came round the corner and ran past Mary, nearly ———— her down.

A knocking   B knocked   C knock

53 Comprehension

In each case, read the passage and then answer the questions about it.

Passage 1

This passage is a true story of a man's bravery.

One day a tea contractor, Mr Chin, was working on an estate in the Cameron Highlands in Malaya. His wife and daughter were helping him to tend young plants and get rid of weeds. While Mr Chin was working, he noticed a movement on the edge of the jungle near the tea plantation.
5   Out of curiosity, he stopped to watch. To his astonishment, a large tigress appeared. It hesitated and then made straight for Mr Chin and his family.

"Quickly!" Mr Chin shouted to his wife and teenage daughter. "Run for the road!"

Mr Chin picked up his parang (a large knife) and turned to face the
10   tigress. He hoped to delay the animal long enough to allow his wife and daughter to escape, but he expected to be killed himself.

The tigress sprang at Mr Chin but he managed to swing his parang and hit it. Both the man and the tigress fell to the ground, unconscious but not fatally wounded. Luckily for Mr Chin, a friend, Mr Pan, was
15   working not far away. Mr Pan heard the noise of the fight, so he went to investigate. He was very surprised to see a tigress on the ground, with Mr Chin lying not far away. Mr Pan picked up his friend and carried him to the road. He managed to stop a helpful motorist, who drove Mr Chin straight to hospital.

20   Mr Pan informed the police. The tigress disappeared but was later hunted down and shot by a Game Ranger, Mohamed Said. The Game Ranger discovered that the tigress had injured a paw in a wire trap and had been forced to chew through its paw to escape from the trap. As a result, it had been unable to hunt wild animals and had attacked Mr Chin
25   when it could not get food in any other way.

The police blamed the man who had set the illegal wire trap but they could not find him. Mr Chin was in hospital for three months but eventually recovered.

1 What made Mr Chin look at the edge of the jungle?

A He wanted to protect his family.

B He heard an unusual noise.

C He happened to see something move there.

D He wanted to see what the tigress was going to do.

2 In line 3 of the passage, we can guess that 'tend' means _____.

A cut down   B look after   C pull out   D tie up

3 How old was Mr Chin's daughter?

A Under fourteen.   C We can't tell.

B Over eighteen.   D Thirteen to nineteen.

4 What was the MAIN reason why Mr Chin stopped to fight the tigress?

A He knew that it was wounded and not very dangerous.

B He hoped to protect his wife and daughter.

C He was too old to run to the road.

D He did not want Mr Pan to feel ashamed of him.

5 How do we know that Mr Chin did not manage to kill the tigress?

A There is no proof of this.

B The tigress did not attack Mr Pan when he went to help.

C The tigress injured a paw in an illegal wire trap.

D A Game Ranger shot and killed the tigress later on.

6 When did Mr Pan go to see what was wrong?

A When he saw the tigress attack Mr Chin.

B When the tigress first came out of the jungle.

C When he saw Mr Chin lying on the ground.

D When he heard the noise of a fight.

7 What effect did the wire trap have on Mr Chin (indirectly)?

A It didn't have any effect on him.

B He injured himself when he was caught in it.

C It stopped the tigress from attacking Mr Chin.

D It probably led the animal to attack and injure Mr Chin.

8 Which of the following titles best sums up the passage?

    A A Brave Man Gives his Life for his Family

    B Tigress Shot by Game Ranger after Thrilling Hunt

    C Contractor Saves Family from Tigress

    D Man Fights Tiger to save his Friends

9 In line 14, 'fatally' is similar in meaning to _____.

    A seriously   C leading to death

    B suddenly   D immediately

10 In line 16, 'investigate' is similar in meaning to _____.

    A give assistance   C fight against

    B find out about   D catch a criminal

11 Why didn't the police blame the tigress for Mr Chin's injuries?

    A They did not see it attack him.

    B They understood why the tigress had attacked him.

    C It was already dead.

    D They did not want to offend animal-lovers.

12 Which of these words is opposite in meaning to 'illegal' in line 26?

    A unlawful   B bad   C harmless   D lawful

Passage 2

Look at this map. It shows:

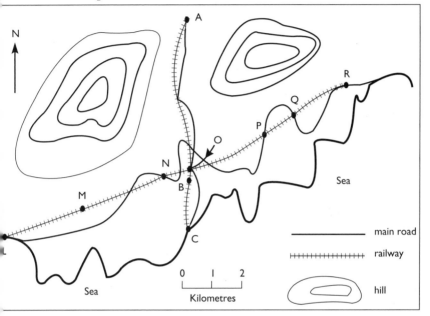

1 main roads from L to R and from A to C

2 a railway line from L to R

3 a railway line from A to C

Study the key and the scale.

Notice the arrow pointing to the north. Below the map you can see railway fares between stations in dollars.

Fares between stations in dollars:

L-M	M-N	N-O	O-P	P-Q	Q-R	A-B	B-C	B-O
1.20	1.00	1.40	1.30	1.00	1.20	2.20	0.90	0.80

Answer these questions about the map.

1 How far is it from B to C by train?

2 Between N and O, which is the longer distance: the railway or the road?

3 Which section of the road is the most winding?

4 If Peter goes from L to C by train, at which station will he prob-ably have to change trains?

197

5 A level-crossing is a place where a railway crosses a road. How many level-crossings are there between L and O? (Assume that there are no bridges.)

6 Write down the fare between O and P in words (and NOT in figures).

7 What is the cost of a return ticket between L and O? Give the answer in figures.

8 Which places will I drive through if I drive from R to C?

9 Susan went from C to B by train. She did some shopping. Then she bought another ticket and went by train to O. She did some more shopping. Then she bought a third ticket and returned to C. How much did she pay altogether for her rides on trains?

10 Which of the places on the map is perhaps the busiest?

11 In which direction does a train go from A to C?

12 Do you think the road and railway go through tunnels between O and A? Give a reason for your answer.

13 Which TWO places may have good harbours?

14 On a map, hills and mountains are shown by _____.

A a straight line

B the symbol also used for a railway

C a dotted line

D contours

Passage 3 | 15 marks

A man wanted to buy a new car. He looked in a motoring magazine and saw this information about some cars.

Make of car:	SPEEDY	WHIZZEL	LYNX	MARTIN	SPECTRE
engine size (cc)	1300	2000	1600	2500	1100
top speed (km/hr)	120	136	124	160	92
km per gallon	50	42	44	36	57
seating	5	6	5	6	4
boot (cu m)	.45	.6	.7	.80	.54
comfort	fair	fair	good	excellent	good
safety	poor	good	v. good	average	fair
appearance	average	good	fair	v. good	average
price ($)	34,980	54,500	42,000	62,450	34,890

Answer these questions about the cars.

1 Which car has the biggest engine?

2 Which car is the slowest?

3 Which vehicle uses most petrol?

4 Which car looks best?

5 Which is the next to cheapest car?

6 In which car can we put most luggage?

7 Which car is safe and looks good?

8 Do you think the Spectre is the cheapest car to run and buy?

9 Which of the two cheap cars is the least safe?

10 Mr Johnson wants to buy a car. He has five people in his family. He wants a car which is safe, comfortable and not too expensive to run. He cannot afford to pay more than $45,000. Which is the best car for him to buy?

11 Which of the cars will be the most expensive to insure? Give a reason for your answer.

12 If the Government decides to add a 10% tax to the price of all new cars, which car will be cheapest?   (2 marks)

13 In the table, 'km per gallon' is used to show how far cars can travel on a gallon of petrol. If we change this to 'miles per litre', which car will be the most expensive to run.
(1 gallon = 4.55 litres. 1 mile = 1.6 km)   (2 marks)

<h2>Passage 4   14 marks</h2>

This bar chart shows the height of children in a class. Look at the chart and then answer the questions about it.

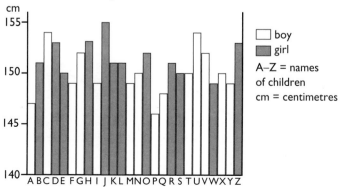

Answer these questions about the bar chart

1 How many children are there in the class?

2 How many of them are girls?

3 Who is the tallest child?

4 Who are the two tallest girls?

5 Who are the two shortest pupils in this class?

6 How many boys are more than 150 cm tall?

7 How many girls are less than 150 cm tall?

8 What is the difference in centimetres between the tallest and the shortest children?

9 How many children are exactly the same height as E?

10 How many girls are taller than the shortest boy?

11 Who are the next to tallest girls?

12 Who is the next to shortest boy?

13 Who is the same height as A?

14 Who are the same height as K?

Passage 5

Look at these two pie charts. They show how much of each $100 a family spends in (a) an urban area (in a town) and (b) a rural area (in the countryside).

Amount of money spent for every $100 received.

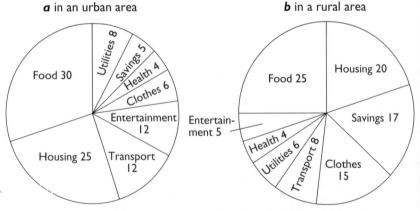

'Utilities' means gas, electricity, water and fuel. It also includes the telephone here.

Answer these questions about the pie charts.

1 Do people in a city spend more or less on entertainment than people in rural villages?

2 Why do people in a town spend more on transport?

3 Why do people in a rural village spend less on housing than city-dwellers do?

4 Think VERY carefully. Do the pie charts mean that rural people spend LESS money each year on utilities than city-dwellers do?

5 Mrs Wilson lives in a town. If she receives $1000 each month, how much does she spend on clothes?

6 Mr King lives in a rural village. If he receives $500 each month, how much does he spend on health?

7 Look at question *5*. How much does Mrs Wilson spend on food each month?

8 Look at question *6*. How much does Mr King spend on food each month?

9 Look at your answers to *7* and *8*. Who spends most money on food in a year?

10 Draw another pie chart for people living between a town and the countryside.

Their figures (per $100) are:

Housing:	35	Clothes:	5
Food:	27	Savings:	5
Transport:	10	Entertainment:	4
Utilities:	10	Health:	4

Passage 6   12 marks

In 1934, the liner 'Morro Castle' caught fire when returning to New York after cruising in the West Indies. Many passengers abandoned the ship in lifeboats. The radio operator, George Rogers, remained at his post, sending out SOS calls until the heat in the radio room became
5 unbearable. Rescue ships arrived, and the 'Morro Castle' was towed into New York harbour, where the fire was finally put out.

134 passengers lost their lives in the disaster but the papers praised

Rogers, who quickly became a hero. He travelled around the USA, earning handsome fees for giving talks about the disaster. On one occasion,
10 Rogers remarked to a police officer that the fire could have been started deliberately by somebody who had left a pen containing concealed explosives in the ship's library.

Gradually attitudes to Rogers began to change. It was discovered that the captain of the ship had found fault with Rogers' work and had told
15 him that his job would cease when the ship returned to port. Shortly afterwards, the captain was taken ill during dinner. He had returned to his cabin and had died in his bath. His body was retained on the ship.

Rogers opened a shop to repair radios, and insured it heavily. Soon afterwards, the shop was destroyed in a mysterious fire, so the
20 insurance company had to pay out. Rogers then joined the New Jersey police force to repair radios. He became envious of a superior officer and planted a bomb in an aquarium in the man's home. The officer lost a finger when the bomb exploded. Rogers was arrested and sent to prison. Shortly after he was released, he had a quarrel with his
25 neighbours and murdered them. He was sent to prison and died there in 1958. Was he a hero or just a cunning murderer?

1 What is the MAIN reason why the fire on the 'Morro Castle' is called a disaster?

A The fire forced some passengers to leave the ship.

B It was probably started deliberately.

C The captain died as a result of it.

D Over 100 people died as a result of it.

2 What forced Rogers to stop sending out radio messages?

A He wanted to escape in a lifeboat.

B His room became too hot for him to continue.

C He had to go to the library to leave an explosive pen there.

D He left to board one of the rescue ships.

3 In line 2, 'abandoned' means …

A leave   C deserted because of the heat
B leaving   D left without intending to return

4 In line 5, 'towed' is similar in meaning to …

A pulled   B helped   C steered   D pushed

5 In line 9, 'handsome' is most similar in meaning to …

   A generous   B beautiful   C pretty   D undeserved

6 Rogers was paid for the talks he gave because …

   A people suspected that he was a criminal

   B there was great interest in the fire on the liner

   C the audience felt sorry for the way he had lost his job

   D his listeners wanted to know what happened inside a prison

7 'Gradually attitudes to Rogers began to change.' We can guess that people became …

   A more understanding   C more suspicious

   B kinder to him   D less hostile

8 Rogers may have started the fire on the 'Morro Castle' deliberately in order to …

   A kill the captain and some of the passengers or crew

   B claim from an insurance company for the damage to the ship

   C destroy any evidence of poison in the captain's body

   D make people think he was a hero

9 In line 19, 'mysterious' suggests that …

   A the cause of the fire was unknown

   B Rogers did not know how the fire started

   C Rogers probably had enemies, who set fire to the shop

   D nobody knew in which year it happened

10 In line 21, 'envious' is similar in meaning to …

   A jealous   B angry   C annoyed   D furious

11 We could say that after the fire in 1934, Rogers' career went …

   A up steadily until he died

   B up and then steadily down

   C down and then steadily up

   D down from the from the time he left the ship

12 It seems from the passage, that Rogers _____ _____ the fire on the 'Morro Castle'.

   A definitely started   C tried to put out

   B did not start   D probably started

Passage 7   12 marks

In the early days of Jamaica, five young Maroon boys went out and used bows and arrows to shoot large birds for food. While they were in the forest, they heard enemy soldiers, the British Redcoats, approaching. The boys camouflaged themselves with leaves so that they looked like bushes.

"Did you count how many soldiers there were?" Tommy asked.

David showed his hands twice. That meant twenty. They waited a few minutes to give the soldiers time to walk past Charlie. When they heard Charlie croaking the frog-signal to them, they rose and hurried
5   back to him. John and Uriah were already in the clearing.

"Did you pick up the arrows and everything else?" Johnny asked.

"Of course. What do you take me for?" said Charlie.

"I hope you did, for one of them is suspicious. He's coming back," John said softly.

10   The boys froze where they were. Then Tommy saw the Redcoat. The soldier picked up something and looked at it. It was an arrow!

The soldier muttered, "It must be an old one. There's nobody here."

If he had been a man of the bush, he would have noticed the fresh scar on the arrow caused by the bowstring when it was released. But he
15   just shrugged his shoulders and turned back to rejoin his companions.

Uriah turned quickly to Charlie.

"So you picked them all up, did you? Would you like to know what we think of you?"

Charlie was ashamed. "I'm sorry," he said. "I – I really thought I'd
20   picked them up."

"You nearly got us all killed or captured," David said. "I don't know how you were made into a young warrior!"

"Stop that!" Tommy said sharply, for he had seen the pain in Charlie's face. He, and Johnny too, knew that Charlie was having his
25   own secret sufferings. Charlie had cheated, and could never forget that he had cheated.

(adapted from *The Young Warriors* by V S Reid)

1 What were the boys doing in the forest?

   A They were running away from their homes.

   B They were hunting for food.

   C They were searching for British soldiers.

   D They were trying to escape from soldiers who were hunting them.

2 In the introduction, 'camouflaged' means ...

   A concealed their appearance

   B made (themselves) smell differently

   C picked or tore off

   D took off and cooked

3 Charlie's frog-signal evidently meant ...

   A Come towards me.   C All clear.

   B Be careful!   D Stop and wait.

4 The arrows in line 6 had probably come from ...

   A the Redcoats or other soldiers

   B adult Maroon warriors

   C somebody who had lost them

   D the boys when they were hunting

5 In line 7, 'take me for' means ...

   A think I am   C expect me to do

   B want me to do   D want to do with me

6 In line 8, 'them' refers to ...

   A the boys   C the arrows

   B the soldiers   D Johnny and Uriah

7 When the soldier returned, he did not notice the boys because ...

   A they had climbed up a tree

   B they looked like part of the forest

   C they were concealed behind boulders

   D he was staring at the ground all the time

8 In line 15, the soldier shrugged his shoulders, showing that ...

   A he was disappointed by what he had found

   B he was impatient to catch up with his companions

   C he saw nothing to make him suspicious

   D he was tired and wanted to sleep

9 What did the boys probably think of Charlie (in line 18)?

   A They thought he was very brave.

   B They thought he was not telling the truth.

   C They thought he had tried to cheat the soldier.

   D They thought he was ashamed of them.

10 Charlie put his friends in danger by ...

   A dropping an arrow on the ground

   B failing to do his duty

   C making a noise which attracted a soldier

   D not counting his arrows correctly

11 In line 19, 'ashamed' is similar in meaning to ...

   A caught trying to deceive other people about something

   B anxious to remain friends with people

   C feeling guilty because of having done something wrong

   D slightly annoyed and trying to defend himself

12 Tommy and Johnny knew that Charlie ...

   A had a guilty conscience

   B would never try to cheat anybody again

   C had not cheated anybody deliberately

   D would soon forget what had happened

Passage 8   10 marks

Annie John is 17. She comes from Antigua and is about to leave for England to become a nurse. Here she is writing about the morning of her last day in Antigua.

I shook myself and prepared to get up. Everything I would do that morning I would be doing for the last time, for I had made up my mind that, come what may, the road for me now went only in one direction: away from home.

5   I bathed quickly and put on my clothes. Along with my earrings, neck chain and bracelets, all made of gold from Guyana, my clothes had been sent to my mother's obeah woman and whatever she had done to my jewellery and clothes would protect me from evil spirits and every kind of misfortune.

At breakfast I was seated in my usual place, with my mother at one
10   end of the table, my father at the other and me in the middle. We were having a Sunday breakfast, as if we had just come from Sunday-morning service: salt fish and sourse and hard-boiled eggs and even special Sunday bread from Mr Daniel, our baker. Sunday breakfast at eleven o'clock was the best breakfast we ate, and the only breakfast better than
15   that was the one we ate on Christmas morning. My parents were in a festive mood, saying what a wonderful time I would have in my new life, and what a lucky person I was. They were eating away as they talked, my father's false teeth making that clop-clop sound like a horse as he talked, my mother's mouth going up and down like a donkey's as she
20   chewed each mouthful thirty-two times. I was looking at them with a smile on my face and disgust in my heart when my mother said, "Of course, you are a young lady now, and we won't be surprised if in due time you write to say that one day soon you are to be married."

Without thinking, I said, with rancour that I didn't hide very well,
25   "How absurd!"

My parents immediately stopped eating and looked at me as if they had not seen me before. Then they went back to their food.

(Adapted from *Annie John* by Jamaica Kincaid)

1 Annie shook herself (in line 1) ...

A to get rid of water on her hair.

B because she had a headache.

C to help her to wake up.

D to show disagreement with somebody.

2 In line 3, 'come what may' is similar in meaning to …

   A regardless of who called to visit her

   B regardless of what might happen

   C if she was allowed to leave

   D if she could obtain permission from her parents

3 We learn from the first paragraph that Annie was determined …

   A to look after herself away from her parents

   B to return home as soon as she could

   C to get married and leave home

   D not to forget her parents when she was away from them

4 It seems likely from the second paragraph that 'obeah' has some connection with …

   A cookery   C funerals

   B lending money   D magic or witchcraft

5 Which two words in lines 10–14 tell us that Annie had NOT just come from a church service?

   A usual place   C just come

   B as if   D best breakfast

6 "My parents were in a festive mood." This suggests that …

   A it was Christmas Day or another special day

   B they were not sorry to see their daughter go overseas

   C they felt sad because Annie would be away for a long time

   D food was the only thing they really cared about

7 The expression 'with a smile on my face and disgust in my heart' makes readers think that Annie was

   A two-faced or a hypocrite

   B worried about something

   C very upset at having to leave her parents

   D less upset than her parents were

208

8 We can guess from Annie's comment that 'rancour' in line 24 probably means something like ...

  A affection   B great love   C cheerfulness D bitterness

9 What effect did Annie's comment (in line 25) have on her parents?

  A It had no effect at all.

  B They were secretly very pleased.

  C They were somewhat shocked at first.

  D They were extremely angry and scolded her immediately.

10 It seems from this passage that Annie's home life had been ...

  A always very happy   C perfect most of the time

  B not very pleasant   D one full of affection

Passage 9   12 marks

One night four bachelors were sleeping soundly in a suburban house which they shared. At about 4.30 a.m. one of them was awakened by the squawking of terrified chickens in their compound. Gunasekaran, 20, jumped out of bed and hurriedly put on his clothes.

5   "Thieves!" he thought. "There must be thieves after our chickens!" He groped round for his torch and then picked up a metal bar.

Gunasekaran banged on the doors of his three friends: Abu Bakar, Kadir and Ismail.

"Quickly!" he shouted to them. "We've got thieves after our chickens!"

10   The three men soon appeared, each carrying a knife or a long piece of wood. Then they rushed outside to search for the thieves. To their astonishment, there was only one thief but it was five metres long and had a chicken in its mouth. The men shone their torches on the largest python they had ever seen. It was as thick round as a man's upper leg

15 and showed no signs of retreating. Meanwhile, chickens rushed madly around everywhere, terrified at the python and the noise.

For the next few minutes, there was a desperate struggle in the darkness. As the snake thrashed about, it knocked Abu Bakar down. He managed to seize its tail and then pin the snake to the ground under the

20 weight of his large body. The other three men stopped the python from reaching back to get at their friend. At one stage, the python managed to coil itself round Gunasekaran's left arm and then tried to wrap itself round his chest to suffocate him. Fortunately, Kadir had a sharp knife. He gave

the snake a quick stab which forced it to release Gunasekaran. Abu Bakar
25 narrowly avoided being bitten before he succeeded in slipping a noose
round the python's head. Gunasekaran and Ismail held onto the rest of
the snake's body. Between them, they managed to lash it to a long pole.

The next morning the men sold the python to a local zoo to compensate them for the loss of two chickens and for damage accidentally
30 done to the hen-house during the struggle. The python shows no signs
of being seriously injured and it eventually settled down at the zoo.

1 In line 1, 'bachelors' are …

  A men who have never married

  B men whose wives have died

  C young unemployed men

  D athletes who take part in competitions

2 Which word suggests that the four men owned the house?

  A soundly   B suburban   C shared   D compound

3 The squawking of the chickens was caused by …

  A joy   B fear   C anger   D hunger

4 In line 6, 'groped' tells us that Gunasekaran …

  A could not see clearly then

  B had no idea where his torch was

  C failed to find his torch

  D went round in a circle

5 When Kadir left the house, he was carrying a …

  A long piece of wood   C rope made into a noose

  B coil of rope or wire   D sharp knife

6 What woke Kadir up at 4.30 a.m.?

  A Some thieves.   C Somebody banging on his door.

  B The noise of the chickens.   D He could not sleep well.

7 Why did Ismail leave the house?

   A He wanted to catch the python.

   B He thought there were thieves outside.

   C He was obeying Gunasekaran's orders.

   D He knew a lot about ways of capturing snakes.

8 Which word in lines 11–13, tells us that the men had not expected to see a python?

   A search   C largest

   B astonishment   D terrified

9 The men struggled to capture the snake …

   A To defend themselves.

   B To sell it at a market.

   C To protect their chickens.

   D To have it for a meal.

10 What did Ismail do in the struggle to capture the snake?

   A He pinned its tail to the ground.

   B He slipped a noose round its head.

   C He used his knife to stab the python.

   D H clung to the body of the snake.

11 In line 23, 'suffocate' is similar in meaning to …

   A crush   C swallow

   B stop (him) from breathing   D bite severely

12 In lines 28-29, 'compensate' is similar in meaning to …

   A make up or balance (for a loss)

   B do something in addition

   C give somebody a reward

   D encourage somebody to do something

Passage 10

(This passage is adapted from *Twenty Thousand Leagues Under the Sea* by Jules Verne. The man telling the story is Professor Aronnax. He is on board a submarine, the '*Nautilus*', commanded by Captain Nemo.)

When I woke up, I found that the '*Nautilus*' was stationary. It was floating on a lake surrounded by a circle of walls two miles in diameter and six in circumference. The walls were like an immense funnel turned upside down, with a height of 500–600 yards. At the summit there was a
5 circular hole through which I saw the gleam of daylight.

"Where are we?" I asked.

"In the very heart of an extinct volcano," Captain Nemo replied. "Its interior was invaded by the sea some time in the past, perhaps after some great disturbance of the earth. While you were sleeping, Professor,
10 the '*Nautilus*' penetrated to this lake through a natural canal which opens about ten yards beneath the surface of the ocean. This place is our harbour of refuge: a mysterious but safe and spacious one, sheltered from all gales."

"Certainly," I replied, "you are in safety here, Captain Nemo. Who could
15 reach you in the heart of a volcano? But didn't I see an opening at its top?"

"Yes, that's the crater, formerly filled with lava, vapour and flames. Now it lets in the air which we all breathe here."

"But what is this volcanic mountain?"

"It belongs to one of the numerous islands dotted about this part of
20 the sea. To vessels it is merely a hill on an uninhabited island but to us it is an immense cavern. I discovered it by chance and it has served us well."

"But how does it help you, Captain?"

"The *Nautilus* needs electricity to make it move, and the fuel to make the electricity – sodium to feed the elements, coal from which to get
25 the sodium, and a coal mine to supply the coal. Exactly at this spot the sea covers entire forests embedded centuries ago and now turned into coal; for me they are an inexhaustible mine."

"Do your men follow the trade of miners here, then?"

"Exactly so. These mines extend under the waves. Here, in their
30 diving dresses, pickaxe and shovel in hand, my men extract the coal, which I do not even ask from the mines of the earth. When I burn the coal to manufacture sodium, the smoke escaping from the crater gives it the appearance of an active volcano."

1 The "I" in line 1 of the passage is …

   A Jules Verne   C Captain Nemo

   B Professor Aronnax   D an unknown person

2 Which word in the first paragraph tells us that the 'Nautilus' was not moving?

   A stationary   B floating   C surrounded   D funnel

3 What sometimes came out of the hole at the summit?

   A A gleam of daylight.   C Molten lava and coal.

   B Smoke from burning coal.   D A great disturbance of some kind.

4 An extinct volcano (line 7) is one which …

   A is extremely large   C is no longer active

   B has a crater at the top   D is an artificial one

5 The harbour of the 'Nautilus' was NOT …

   A unusual   B man-made   C safe   D sheltered

6 Sea entered the inside of the volcano …

   A through a hole at the top

   B by means of the summit

   C along a channel made by Captain Nemo

   D along a natural route under the surface

7 Air entered the natural harbour …

   A through the hollow crater

   B when coal was burnt to produce oxygen

   C through a natural canal beneath the surface of the sea

   D by means of underground pipes

8 Strangers sailing past the mountain might think it was simply …

   A an island with a few people on it

   B a naval harbour for ships and submarines

   C a volcano which was sometimes active and sometimes inactive

   D a military base of some kind

9 Before Captain Nemo could get sodium, ...

    A he had to obtain coal   C he had to feed the elements

    B he had to pay for it   D he needed a supply of
                                                 hydrogen

10 Captain Nemo thought that his supply of coal ...

    A would last for ever

    B would not last long

    C depended on mines on land

    D was in danger of disappearing

54 Cloze Passages

Sometimes you may have to fill in blank spaces in a passage. Then you can follow these guidelines:

1 **Use the right part of speech.** Decide whether to use a noun, an adjective, an adverb or another part of speech.

Exercise 1

Choose the right words from the brackets.

1 Mary is going to take her driving test tomorrow. I hope she will be _____ .

(succeed, success, successful, successfully)

2 She is sure that she will _____ in passing the test.

(succeed, success, successful, successfully)

3 Mary is not _____ . In fact, she works very hard.

(lazy, laziness, lazily)

4 Sometimes workers lose their jobs because of their _____ .

(lazy, laziness, lazily)

5 Mr King smiled _____ when he heard that he had been promoted.

(happy, happiness, happily)

6 What's the _____ between these two words?

(differently, different, difference)

7 This word is used in a _____ way.

(differently, different, difference)

8 We must find out the _____ time of Uncle's plane.

(arrive, arrived, arriving, arrival)

9 This road is not _____ enough, so the Government is going to _____ it soon.

(wide, widely, width, widen)

10 Susan _____ recovered from her illness.

(quick, quickness, quickly)

2 Use a word which fits the meaning of the expression or sentence.

Exercise 2

Choose the right words from the brackets.

1 Peter went to see a doctor yesterday. _____ gave him some medicine, so he thanked her.

(He, She, I)

2 Vehicles must stop when the traffic lights change to _____ .

(green, pink, blue, yellow, red)

3 A bear chased some children round a house but failed to catch _____ .

(it, him, her, they, them, us)

4 When Mary saw that a child was drowning, she jumped into the _____ to rescue him. She was surprised to find that the water in the lake was extremely cold.

(sea, swimming-pool, steam, lake, river, pond)

5 When Peter saw that a child was drowning, he _____ into the swimming-pool and nearly hit his head on the bottom.

(waded, dived, jumped)

3 Use a word which fits the structure or pattern of the sentence.

Exercise 3

Choose the right words from the brackets.

1 Do you think Mary is _____ of passing her driving test at her first attempt?

(capable, able, going)

2 Yes, I expect she will pass _____ her first attempt.

(on, in, by, at, with)

3 We have lived here _____ early in 1990.

(for, past, since)

4 Mary is not only pretty _____ kind and friendly too.

(but, and, also)

5 _____ an hour for a bus is a waste of time.

(Wait, Wait, Waiting, waiting)

Exercise 4

Choose the most suitable word(s) to complete the sentences.

1 Uncle is more than an hour late. It looks as _____ he is not going to come.

A long　　　　B like　　　　C how　　　　D if

2 You can go to your friend's home as long _____ you return by 9 p.m.

A as　　　　B if　　　　C though　　　　D but

3 Please give this letter to Miss Nathan when you _____ her tomorrow.

A see　　　　B saw　　　　C seeing　　　　D will see

4 Hurry up! It's time we _____ for the station to meet Uncle and Aunty.

A leave　　　　B left　　　　C have left　　　　D will leave

5 Have you _____ to Susan's letter yet?

A answered　　　　B written　　　　C replied　　　　D dealt with

6 Mary: Do you know _____ Mummy is now?
　Paul: Yes, she's at the market.

A how　　　　B what　　　　C when　　　　D where

7 When you buy new shoes, make sure they are the right _____ .

A fitness　　　　B size　　　　C measure　　　　D heel

8 Peter had to stay in hospital for a fortnight. He was really _____ when he was able to go home.

A joyfully　　　　B lovely　　　　C please　　　　D glad

9 When you travel on a bus or train, you must pay your _____ .

A journey　　　　B fare　　　　C fee　　　　D ticket

10 Mary is going to a wedding tomorrow, so she wants to _____ her best dress.

A dress　　　　B used　　　　C wear　　　　D do

Exercise 5

Choose the most suitable word(s) to complete the sentences.

1 It rained heavily last night, so we _____ to postpone our Sports Meeting for a week.

   A decided   B said   C told   D concluded

2 We were late for school yesterday. The reason for the delay _____ that the road was blocked when a tree was blown down.

   A why   B because   C being   D was

3 Mary has invited us to her party but we cannot _____ her invitation because we have to stay at home on that day.

   A respond   B agree   C except   D accept

4 Uncle is coming here next month. He wants us to _____ two rooms for him and his family.

   A order   B write   C book   D preserve

5 Mary always wears slippers on the beach _____ she will not cut her feet on glass.

   A unless   B since   C because   D so that

6 The meeting of the Chess Club has been _____ for a week because some members have influenza.

   A cancelled   B abolished   C postponed   D reserved

7 Peter: Can you lend me twenty dollars?
Mary: No, you _____ me fifty dollars already.

   A owe   B own   C due   D borrowed

8 My grandfather will be 65 soon, so he is going to _____ from his job and stay at home.

   A retire   B dismiss   C retreat   D sack

9 The manager scolded Peter because he was not _____ with Peter's work.

   A satisfactory   B satisfying   C satisfy   D satisfied

10 I could not sleep last night because it was _____ a hot night.

   A very   B such   C so   D too

11 (In a shop) I like this dress and I want to buy it but it's a bit loose just here. Could you _____ it for me, so that it fits properly?

   A alter   B mend   C stitch   D adapt

12 I must go to the dentist tomorrow. When I was eating an apple this morning, one of my _____ came out. Now I've got a hole in one of my teeth.

   A stoppers   B gums   C fillings   D extractions

Exercise 6

On the lines at the right, write ONE word which we can use in the blank space. Number 1 is done as an example.

A Diary

18 September: Miss King, our English teacher said that we (**1**) _____ keep a diary so that we can (**2**) _____ our English. Now I am starting my diary. This morning my friend and I managed to get 19 marks (**3**) _____ of 20 in a mathematics test at school. I had a (**4**) _____ of homework to do, (**5**) _____ I could not watch my favourite TV programmes.

(**1**) _____must_____

(**2**) _____

(**3**) _____

(**4**) _____

(**5**) _____

20 September: Yesterday evening I (**6**) _____ to write in my diary. Uncle and Aunty came to visit us. They (**7**) _____ us out to dinner. After dinner (**8**) _____ all went to a local cinema. I did not go to bed (**9**) _____ quite late, so I felt very tired this morning.

(**6**) _____

(**7**) _____

(**8**) _____

(**9**) _____

21 September: A horrible day! All the (**10**) _____ were out of (**11**) _____, so we had to walk up and down fifteen very steep flights of (**12**) _____ . Daddy was in a rather bad temper for part of the evening, so I (**13**) _____ the dog out for a long walk to help him. Even the dog looked quite tired (**14**) _____ it had walked up all the stairs. Grandpa (**15**) _____ not go out at all. He said he wished we (**16**) _____ on the first or second floor. We all agreed (**17**) _____ him.

(**10**) _____

(**11**) _____

(**12**) _____

(**13**) _____

(**14**) _____

(**15**) _____

(**16**) _____

(**17**) _____

22 September: It rained (**18**) _____ all the morning, which was good because the farmers needed rain for (**19**) _____ crops. Some of the water will go into the main (**20**) _____ and increase our supply of water.

(**18**) _____

(**19**) _____

(**20**) _____

Exercise 7

On the lines at the right, write ONE word which we can use in the blank space. (Somebody is speaking to a clerk in a travel agency. The conversation is on the telephone. C – a clerk   T – a traveller.)

T: Hello, is (**1**) _____ the Big World Modern Travel Agency?

(**1**) _____

C: Yes, that's (**2**) _____ . Can I help you?

(**2**) _____

T: I hope (**3**) _____ . I'm planning a visit to Europe with my family.

(**3**) _____

I wonder if you can give me some (**4**) _____ about our trip.

(**4**) _____

C: Yes, certainly. What (**5**) _____ you like to know?

(**5**) _____

T: Well, everything really. I'm not sure how (**6**) _____ it costs to fly there at this (**7**) _____ of the year or how much it will cost us to (**8**) _____ at a decent hotel in Europe. Which are the (**9**) _____ interesting places to visit?

(**6**) _____
(**7**) _____
(**8**) _____

(**9**) _____

C: How long do you expect to stay (**10**) _____ Europe?

(**10**) _____

T: That (**11**) _____ on the cost but about two weeks, as far as I can say at the moment. If the hotel charges are (**12**) _____ we may have to (**13**) _____ the trip to 10 days.

(**11**) _____

(**12**) _____
(**13**) _____

C: Well, there are several different (**14**) _____ of flying there, and I can certainly (**15**) _____ some interesting places to visit. Would you like to (**16**) _____ a tour? Then you can travel (**17**) _____ other people. We use a chartered flight, so the fare is lower (**18**) _____ on a scheduled flight.

(**14**) _____
(**15**) _____

(**16**) _____
(**17**) _____

(**18**) _____

T: Are chartered planes (**19**) _____ safe?

(**19**) _____

C: Oh, yes, (**20**) _____ . They are the same planes and pilots as on normal scheduled flights but they go at different times.

(**20**) _____